• STACKPOLE CRIME LIBRARY •

# DEADLY PURSUIT

• STACKPOLE CRIME LIBRARY •

# DEADLY PURSUIT

## Robert V. Cox

STACKPOLE
BOOKS

Originally published in 1977 by Cameron House,
an imprint of Stackpole Books

Copyright © 1977 by Robert V. Cox

This edition published in 2008 by
STACKPOLE BOOKS
5067 Ritter Road
Mechanicsburg, PA 17055
www.stackpolebooks.com

Some of the names of the people involved in the story have been
changed to protect the innocent. However, all events are factual.

Printed in the United States of America

10  9  8  7  6  5  4  3  2  1

Cover photograph by Alan Wycheck
Cover design by Caroline Stover

**Library of Congress Cataloging-in-Publication Data:**

Cox, Robert V.
    Deadly pursuit.
    1.Kidnapping-Pennsylvania-Case Studies. I. Title.
HV6603.B7C68    1977
364.1'54'0924                            [B]  77-76-773

ISBN 0-8117-0481-5 HC edition
ISBN 978-0-8117-3522-3 PB edition

*To Martha and Phyllis*

# ACKNOWLEDGMENTS

The author wishes to thank John C. Staley, J. Michael Anderson, Barbara Norville, and Leslie Fleisher Schwartz for their editorial assistance. Special thanks is given to Kenneth L. Peiffer, Jr. who not only shared many of the experiences with the author and provided a pictorial account of the events, but whose individual experiences are recounted in this work.

# PREFACE

When I decided to tell the story of *Deadly Pursuit*, of the two years of stark terror which gripped an entire community in a rural area of South Central Pennsylvania, I chose a style which was unique, and at the same time, necessary.

I have had the pleasure of working with police on many investigations for more than two decades while with the news media, and became close friends with many truly remarkable law enforcement personnel.

The format came only after I experienced with investigators, and on my own, the frustrations, thankless efforts, and sometimes perils, that go into the stories behind the stories in the newspapers.

It was impossible to be friends with lawmen, to share their dangers, their triumphs and disappointments, to break bread with them and hoist a glass with them during these times, and then forget them.

It was in this vein, then, that I decided *Deadly Pursuit* would be different.

There would be no one "hero" or "heroine" in the story, since, as usually true in real life, no such person exists.

I decided to let the pursuit carry the trail of terror from its beginning to end, the way most events occur in life. I included the mistakes as well as the proper conclusions made by those involved.

In covering the story for the newspapers, I gained the confidence of the people of the valley, and a first-hand knowledge of the events as they occurred. In some instances, I received calls of attacks before the police did. This happened especially after the first year when the victims felt police were not pressing the investigation to the fullest.

It was with this background that I was able to cover the final incident in the story, the kidnapping of Mary Lou Broderick, to the extent that it earned me the Pulitzer Prize in 1967.

Here then, is the story as it unfolded, through the eyes of those who experienced it.

# PROLOGUE

# VIOLA JACKA   *April 6, 1964*

Viola Jacka lived alone. A widow, with no family nearby, she had a small house in the remote wooded area between Shade Gap and Orbisonia, Pennsylvania. Viola was accustomed to seclusion, but not this strange sense of isolation. She had the feeling of being watched, an eerie sensation that defied explanation.

It was getting late. Viola told herself that sleep might ease her fears. She turned off all the lights except the lamp over the desk in the living room and made her way upstairs toward her bedroom. But halfway up her uneasiness grew and she turned and went back to the dimly-lit living room.

She was now near tears. Not from fear alone, but from anger within herself. Here she was—a grown woman, fifty-one years old, who had lived through many times in which fear had reason to grip her. She had watched her husband die of an incurable disease. She had watched over her children until they were grown. She had lived with fear—but always fear for someone else. Now it was for herself, unreasonable, without cause, and oppressive.

She sat on the sofa for a long time, trying to shake the feeling. She finally gave in and fell into an uneasy sleep. Every breeze rustling tree branches woke her. She dozed fitfully throughout the night.

Morning brought relief. At first light, Viola dressed, prepared for the day ahead and her mile-long walk into town. Moving through her house, she found nothing out of place—nothing to give credence to her strange feelings of the previous night.

Outside, she looked over the house, behind bushes and shrubs, around the trees and still found nothing. Her tension subsided; she left for work.

All day Monday she kept busy and gratefully accepted the offer to spend the night in town. By Tuesday, she was anxious to return home, and walked back there, taking care to arrive before dark.

Turning down the steep dirt road which led to her house, Viola again felt the same unease that had gripped her Sunday night. She imagined creatures lurking in trees and on top of the abandoned railroad bed which paralleled the road. By the time she reached her house she was running, almost slipping on the gravel road. She kept looking back to see if she were being followed. At the door, she jammed her key into the lock and went quickly inside. Slamming the door behind her, she said aloud, "I feel foolish." It didn't help.

For several hours she did her housework and chores by rote—cleaning, washing, cooking, eating. She decided that only by keeping herself occupied would she calm down. After dinner she worked on a plaited rug, turned on the radio, and lost track of time.

As the radio announcer gave the 9:30 station break, all reason left Viola, for outside the house came the sound of a crash followed by a heavy thud against the side of the house. Viola immediately turned off the light in the living room, throwing the house into darkness. She fell into a chair and heard nothing but the music from the radio. She groped for the knob and turned it off.

The only sounds now came from her own breathing and the beating of her heart. She tiptoed to the window on the north side of the house. Through a crack beside the blind she peered out but saw nothing. She held the position for a long time until a car passed on the highway. Then she moved silently to the opposite side of the room to another window facing a quarry and the lights of her nearest neighbor's home, half a mile away. Not a sound came from outside, not a movement. She stayed at the window, then, exhausted, moved back to the sofa. Only after hours of listening did she sleep.

On Wednesday morning, Viola rose and prepared to walk to town. Before leaving her home this time, she discovered a bucket overturned on the side lawn. That night and Thursday passed without incident. She was almost convinced that her fears were unfounded.

Viola's date on Friday evening was just what she needed. She welcomed company after her long, vigilant week. Her date picked her up and they drove leisurely to the American Legion Hall in Orbisonia where they shared a few drinks and watched television.

At 9:30, Viola's date left her at the door of her isolated house. He returned to the Legion Hall.

Alone, Viola nearly forgot her fears of the week and felt only a slight twinge of fear after reading the story of a murder in Philadelphia in the local newspaper. A woman of regular habits, she checked the time, laid down the paper at 10:10 P.M. and moved from the sofa to the vanity dresser she had converted from a desk. She stood in front of the dresser, removed her street clothes and donned a robe before starting to set her hair in curlers.

Her robe was loosely draped over her shoulders and her hands were on top of her head, when a large rock crashed through the living room window, striking the table in the center of the room. The sound of shattering glass and the rattling of the window blind flying unrestrained around its roller were joined instantly by her scream. The scream attracted the attention of a dog in the distance. It answered with a howl. Closer now, with the mournful wail still carrying over the mountainside, the yelping of a puppy joined in the din.

She leaped from her chair at the dresser, knocking it backwards. Immediately a voice outside the shattered window called out, "Don't scream or I'll shoot you."

Numb with fear, she ran from the dresser to the table, keeping away from the window. She stopped and watched in horror as a gun barrel poked through the space of broken glass.

Methodically, the barrel cleared away the broken frame, sweeping clear the slivers and debris. It was then Viola saw the face, partially covered with a Halloween mask. The face contorted when the aiming sight of the gun barrel became tangled in the lace curtain. As the intruder attempted to shake the gun free, he revealed missing teeth in the right side of his mouth. She screamed again and the man withdrew the gun, the curtains following the barrel outside.

Running to the opposite side of the room, she picked up the telephone receiver and tried to reach the operator but her shaking hands could not dial.

Again she screamed as a shot from the gun, inserted once more into the window, shattered the plaster six inches from her head.

"Quit screaming or I'll kill you," the intruder commanded.

All reason left her. She screamed, falling to her knees and crawling away from the spot where the bullet had sunk into the wall. She had reached the center of the room when a second shot was fired. This time the bullet struck a large flower pot, sending crockery, dirt and flowers all over the room.

Silence.

Still on her hands and knees beside the table, Viola raised her head slightly to glance toward the window. She saw nothing but the curtains which moved with the draft. She waited, then crawled across the room toward the opening.

Rising to her feet beside the window frame, she reached

over her head and drew the shade down over the frame. Then she sank to a crouch and moved around the room. In the background she was aware that the radio was playing a folk tune. She skirted the center table to reach the sofa. She reached for her purse on the table, removed the cash and put it under a pillow on the sofa. Satisfied the intruder would not get her money, she stood up and closed her loose house-coat.

Turning slowly, she gazed at the mess of shattered glass, crockery pieces, and the overturned chair. Now she was angry, as well as scared. The only weapon she could think of was a baseball bat left behind by her son. She found it in the living room closet.

She wrapped a towel around her head, then cautiously moved toward the front door, carrying her purse in one hand and the bat in the other. As silently as possible, she un-locked the door.

Only then did she remember that she had left the light on. She quickly crossed the room again, turned off the light and radio, picked up a flashlight from the dresser, and walked back across the darkened room to the front door.

Turning the knob, she peeked out through a small open-ing but saw nothing except the dirt road and trees beyond the railroad bed. Quickly she opened the door and stepped onto the porch. For some unknown reason, she felt com-pelled to lock the door behind her, forgetting that the in-truder had only to lift himself through an open window.

Stepping off the porch, she started to circle the house, holding the purse in the crook of her left arm and the unlit flashlight in her left hand. She carried the baseball bat high above her head with her right hand and made her way toward the window where the gunman had stood. Staying in position for nearly a minute, she attempted to adjust her eyes to the dark.

Something cold touched her bare leg below the knee. She screamed. Wheeling around, she snapped on the flashlight, and was about to bring the bat down when the light revealed a puppy at her feet.

She was reaching for the dog when from across the un-paved road on the railroad bed came a trail of unintelligible sounds. Snapping off the flashlight, she quickly circled to the back of the house, heading in the direction of her nearest neighbor.

The gunman was not fooled. He followed her progress by moving along in the same direction. Her eyes followed his gliding silhouette. When she reached the unpaved road near the side of her home, he called out, "Stop or I'll shoot you!"

Responding directly for the first time, she countered with, "There he is, on top of the railroad. Shoot him, I.D.!" The initials were her brother's.

She started running toward the home of her neighbor, Mary Holden, yelling again and again, "Shoot him, shoot him!" No shots were fired at her as she ran, stumbled and crawled toward Mrs. Holden's.

She fell, skinning her knees and hands, dropping the flashlight and ball bat. But she arose almost in the same motion, picked up the flash and the bat, and started out again.

At last she stumbled onto the front porch of the Holden home, burst through the unlocked door, and collapsed onto the living room floor, sending the bat and flashlight spin-ning across the room.

"Viola, what happened? Are you all right?" Mrs. Holden asked, startled.

After a short rest Viola was able to tell of the attack. Her fear prompted both Mrs. Holden and her son-in-law into action. While Mrs. Holden drew the shades, her son-in-law found a hunting rifle and loaded it. He then took a position by a window in the living room while Mrs. Holden bathed and dressed the brush-burns and cuts on Viola's legs and hands and discussed plans to get help.

Now exhaustion caught up with Viola. She fought back tears as she realized she had forgotten her eyeglasses. They were home on the vanity dresser.

While the son-in-law stood guard at the window, Viola

and Mrs. Holden made plans. They would drive Viola to her home to pick up her glasses and since Mrs. Holden didn't have a telephone, call her daughter and son-in-law from there.

Darkening the farm house before leaving, the trio took turns at windows peering outside. For more than fifteen minutes whispered conversations among the three were the only sounds.

Finally, assured that the gunman was not waiting, they made their move. Led by Mrs. Holden's son-in-law holding the rifle, the two women ran to the car. Both Viola and Mrs. Holden leaped into the back seat while the son-in-law ran around to the driver's side. He opened the car door and squatted down as low as possible behind the wheel.

In a short time they were at the Jacka house. Still behind the wheel, the son-in-law took the safety catch off the gun, cocked the firing mechanism, and pointed the weapon out the window toward the railroad bed. The two women stepped from the car on the passenger's side and ran to the door, lighting the way with flashlights. After what seemed to be an unreasonable time, Viola slid the key into the lock and pushed open the door. Shining the flashlight ahead of her, she played the beam around the room.

Everything was as she had left it—broken glass on the floor near the window, the overturned chair, the rock on the floor, shattered plaster, scattered flowers, dirt and pieces of crockery.

A numbing cold swept over Mrs. Jacka, brought on by her lack of clothing and a new, growing fear. She walked over to the telephone which was still off the hook and held the receiver to her ear. But in spite of every effort, she could not control her hand to dial the number. Sobbing, Viola ran to the dresser, picked up her glasses and put them on.

"Let's go to town and make the call," she pleaded with her neighbor. Mrs. Holden agreed.

Crossing the room, she stopped at the sofa. Reaching under the pillow, she found the money where she had left it. Back at the doorway, she again played the flashlight over the damage. Stepping out onto the front porch, Mrs. Holden called out to her son-in-law, "Is it safe to leave?" He waved them on.

Viola Jacka once again locked the door behind her. They ran to the car and climbed into the back seat.

It took only a minute to drive the short distance to Orbisonia, and the home of Viola's boyfriend. This time all three left the car with the motor still running and ran to the house.

When he opened the door, everyone began to talk at once. Finally he pieced the story together and telephoned Viola's son-in-law.

When he arrived, Viola retold her experience and the son-in-law telephoned the state police substation at Huntingdon. The call was recorded by the officer on duty at 1:10 A.M. Trooper Carl F. Ruegg was radio-dispatched to Orbisonia. He arrived at 1:45 A.M.

After Ruegg heard the story, he directed the group to follow him to the Jacka residence. En route he placed a radio call for assistance.

Four cars were now in the entourage which moved out of Orbisonia toward the isolated home.

When the vehicles stopped in front of the Jacka home, the drivers left the headlights on to illuminate the area.

Gun in hand, the trooper unlocked the house and turned on the lights of the living room. Exhausted by her experience and weary from strain, Viola enacted the incident with Trooper Ruegg. Then she and the trooper began a search of the grounds. Care was taken to remain clear of the area below the shattered window in order to preserve footprints.

Other investigators arrived before daybreak and the grounds were searched again. One of the troopers in the investigation team found the puppy which had frightened Mrs. Jacka the night before. Another trooper found an ejected shell from a .22 caliber weapon outside the shattered windowpane. Fingerprint experts attempted to lift smudges from the window frame and throughout the house. No prints were found that could be traced to anyone other than Mrs. Jacka. Efforts to locate the bullet which had smashed into the wall were unsuccessful.

Mrs. Jacka, calmer now with a half-dozen policemen on the premises, gave a description of the gunman.

He was about five feet, eight or nine inches tall. His voice had no discernible accent. She further described the gunman, from seeing only part of his face at the window, as more than thirty years old. The Halloween mask he wore was of the common variety that could be purchased anywhere.

One other piece of information she recalled was that a car sped away from the main highway while she was running to the home of Mrs. Holden.

The only facts reached in the entire Jacka investigation were that the gunman was an outstanding woodsman, was intimately familiar with the area, and knew how to remove all traces of evidence. Police theorized that he was a Shade Gap resident and that he had, in all probability, stood outside the window of Mrs. Jacka's home many times over the weeks leading up to the shooting.

Trooper Ruegg, questioning the residents in the area, was told by a fifteen-year-old boy that he and his younger brother were alone in their home during the incident. He had heard the shooting, he said.

Further questioning of the boy, however, revealed his initial version of the incident to be misleading. He was taken to headquarters at Huntingdon for further interrogation.

Shortly after questioning began, the boy told police he had an important statement to make.

"I'm the one you want. I'm the gunman. I did it!" the youth told the investigators.

A full statement was taken in the presence of witnesses and signed by the youth in the presence of his parents. It, too, carried discrepancies which led the police to believe that the boy was lying.

On April 24, just two weeks after the shooting, a Huntingdon County Juvenile Court judge ruled that the youth had lied and that he was not the gunman. In his ruling, the judge took into consideration the fact that the youth failed to know all the details of the incident, which proved him to be only an innocent, but disturbed, attention-seeker. The only connection the youth had with the case was the puppy involved. It was his.

Once more police returned to the task of finding the gunman. In all, eighteen residents of the area were questioned.

Investigators assigned to the crime from headquarters in Harrisburg were just as unsuccessful in their probes. The gunman had vanished.

# ANNE WEAVER   *June 1, 1964*

Anne Weaver was comfortable. Although Monday had been exceptionally cold, windy, and rainy, her house trailer was warm and cozy, protecting her from the elements.

At forty-nine, Anne looked far younger, with a trim figure and dark, wavy hair. Full of energy, she decided to start a new project and set about to varnish a flower stand. At 11:15 P.M., she finished her work, gathered her garbage and prepared to throw everything out.

Picking up a flashlight, she stepped out of the kitchen and onto the patio. The night was very dark, the fog was settling in rapidly. Anne wasn't sure she could even find the trash can.

Playing her flashlight on the walk, she had nearly reached her goal when she heard a noise. Thinking that it was a rabbit, she turned the flashlight in the direction of the sound. The beam showed a pair of boot-clad feet. Moving the beam upward, she saw a khaki raincoat and a dark stocking covering the head of a man. Sharp, piercing blue eyes glared menacingly through the slits cut in the mask.

Anne Weaver screamed, but instinctively took the measure of the man standing before her. He was slightly taller than she, and she was five feet, seven inches tall. He seemed bald, but that could have been the stocking over his head. He was carrying a rifle in his right hand.

She screamed again, louder than before. The expression in the man's eyes never changed. Anne whirled around and ran, realizing that she would not be able to reach the door in time. She screamed again, and started to skirt the side of the building when strong arms wrapped around her shoulders from behind. The barrel of the rifle struck her on the face.

"Don't scream, I won't hurt you!" the man said.

She struggled to get free but his fingers sank deeper into her flesh. Again she screamed, this time spinning on her heels and breaking free. But as she moved, he swung the gun barrel in an arc and brought it down on the back of her head.

Pain shot through her, nearly blotting out consciousness. She sank to both knees and fell onto her hands. This time the man yelled, "Don't scream, I'm not going to hurt you!" But she was too scared to listen. She rose on unsteady feet, screamed again as loudly as she could, and started to run toward the highway. Her movement carried her along the side of her house where she saw the lights of neighboring homes barely visible in the fog.

Running close behind her, the man swung the rifle again, this time striking her right shoulder. The force of the blow glanced off her spine, scraping the skin. Falling to the ground, she rolled onto her back, trying to ward off other blows with her hands and arms.

In an instant, he was over her. "Shut up . . . don't scream!"

Another scream followed his warning. This time the unexpected sound echoed between nearby homes and a light went on. The gunman hesitated. Taking advantage of his momentary pause, Anne rolled onto her stomach, and screamed again. She rose and started to run toward the highway, holding the flashlight to the back of her head to protect it from another blow which she felt was sure to come. It never did.

Instead, the man grasped her right arm from behind. His grip tightened as he attempted to pull her backwards to the ground. But her forward motion, given impetus by a stumble which caused her to fall, broke the grasp. She screamed again.

New-found hope gave her the strength to rise and continue her dash towards safety. Now other lights from homes across the highway were being turned on as neighbors woke up.

Still screaming as she ran, she crossed the highway and fell as she reached the yard of her employer. Recovering quickly, she stumbled the remaining distance across the lawn to the front door. She had pounded on the door only once when it swung open. Crying, she fell forward into the living room. Blood from her wounds mixed with tears as she tried to wipe her eyes.

Behind her, Hart, the owner of the house, slammed the door shut and pushed the bolt into place. Then he turned toward the injured woman and checked the gash on her head. While his wife was cleaning the wounds, Hart pieced together the story of the attack and telephoned state police at Huntingdon.

At 11:25 P.M. Trooper Peter Migatulski was dispatched to the Hart home.

Meanwhile Anne Weaver became nauseous and light-headed from pain and fear. The Harts helped her to a couch in the living room. Unable to stem the flow of blood from the woman's head wound, Hart told his wife to hold a compress on the gash while he went to get help from a nurse, Mrs. Helen Locke, who lived only a few doors away.

When the nurse arrived, she succeeded in controlling the blood flow. But realizing the possibility of a skull fracture or brain concussion, she telephoned the Huntingdon Hospital and directed the night clerk to notify the woman's physician.

Anne Weaver was stretched out on the back seat of Hart's

car when Trooper Migatulski arrived. After brief question-ing, Hart drove the injured woman, accompanied by Nurse Locke, thirty miles to the hospital.

Helped by neighbors who were now on the scene, Trooper Migatulski began a search of the area, but was soon forced to stop because of the fog.

One neighbor said he saw a vehicle drive away from the scene and head in a northerly direction toward Orbisonia. It could have been a 1956 model Chevrolet, he told the inves-tigator.

By dawn, Trooper Migatulski was aided in his investiga-tion by other officers from Huntingdon. An inch-by-inch search of the area behind the Arnold trailer revealed foot-prints made by someone wearing snow boots or galoshes. The prints led across the cornfield from behind the Hart Market, directly to the trash can where the initial attack had occurred. The tracks then followed the path Anne Weaver had fled, but were lost in an alley nearby. Plaster casts were secured but other imprints made by well-meaning residents made identification impossible.

Late in the afternoon, Anne Weaver was discharged from the Huntingdon Hospital. It had taken a number of sutures to close the wound on her head.

Word of the Weaver attack spread quickly throughout Shade Gap. Investigators increased their activity in the area, tracking down all rumors of peeping Tom incidents. Seven new suspects in the case were questioned but police were unable to find any concrete evidence to place charges.

Police theorized that the attack was made by a man famil-iar with the area and known to his victim. But Anne Weaver steadfastly denied knowing anyone with such outstanding eyes. The average height and build of the attacker could have fit the description of more than half the residents of the area.

In an attempt to link the attacker of Anne Weaver with the gunman who had shot at Viola Jacka, police cross-checked the descriptions given by both women. The only difference in the two descriptions was the eyes, which were hidden behind a mask in the Jacka incident.

The police assumption that the same man was guilty of both crimes was shared by the inhabitants of the valley. A self-imposed curfew was immediately adopted and night-time activity came to an abrupt halt. Children normally unafraid of the dark suddenly were anxious to be home before sundown.

# MARTHA I. YOHN  *July 1, 1964*

The people of Shade Gap tried to resume their normal life style. School was over and the care of planted fields was uppermost in everyone's mind. Logging operations in the valley were at a high mark.

The state park at Cowan's Gap, eight miles away, was the favorite spot for the families of the area to spend leisure time. Standing at the kitchen stove of her new mobile home north of Neelyton, Martha I. Yohn was making plans for an outing for the weekend. It was only Wednesday, but her husband's unexpected arrival home, just an hour before, gave her the opportunity to approach him with the idea.

Charles Yohn's work as a truck driver kept him away from home all week. Today, however, he told her that he would be back again by the weekend.

Only nineteen years old, the attractive mother of a thirteen-month-old son could hardly wait to take a day's vacation from her household chores.

The telephone rang. The call was for Martha from her sister, Mrs. Ruth Snyder, who lived south of Neelyton. Mrs.

Snyder had some cherries for her sister and wanted her to pick them up that evening. Martha agreed.

Charles said he would like to visit some of his friends, rather than ride with his wife to her sister's home. His friends would drive him home later, he said.

Shortly after 6 P.M., Martha dropped him off at a service station in Neelyton where he met his friends. With her son Craig on the front seat beside her, she continued on to her sister's home.

It was not yet 6:30 P.M. when she arrived.

The talk between the two sisters naturally centered on the two previous attacks on women in nearby Shade Gap. But this was a warm summer evening and any thought of a third attack seemed remote. The attacks were both on older women and were concentrated north and west of the location of the Snyder farm.

"Another thing, they were both late at night, long after dark," Martha said while glancing out the kitchen window into the early evening. It was nearly 7:30 P.M. when she rose to leave, picking Craig off the floor where he was playing.

Martha placed the child on the front seat of the car, walked around and got in behind the wheel. Before driving away, she gave her son his nursing bottle.

She had driven only a half mile when a sight on the road ahead caused her to brake suddenly. Her right hand automatically shot out to her son to keep him from falling from the seat. Surprise, not fear, registered in her at what she saw. The highway was blocked by logs from a pile along the side of the road. Someone could get hurt by a trick like that, she thought. Annoyance rose up in her.

"Just suppose someone would have come along here driving real fast," she said to her infant son who was contentedly drawing on the nipple of the bottle. "There could have been an awful wreck." She started to leave the car to remove the logs from the road.

What she saw next made her remove her hand from the door handle and hesitate only a moment before taking decisive action.

Suddenly appearing on a six-foot embankment along the right side of the road was a man carrying a high-powered rifle. That in itself was not strange in this mountainous area, but with temperatures still in the 80's, the man's appearance stopped her cold.

He had a beard that looked as if it was more than two weeks old and wore a full-length heavy brown overcoat and arctic boots that were unbuckled. His eyes were exceptionally large and shaded from the evening sun by a bright red baseball cap. He had a large protruding chin. His eyes were fixed on Martha as he jumped from the embankment onto the highway at the point of the barricade.

She was horrified as she realized she was facing the man who had attacked the two women in Shade Gap. She was defenseless, isolated from everyone, and had her infant son lying on the car seat beside her.

Quickly she put the car into reverse while keeping her eyes glued to the man who was slowly approaching the car. She had chosen a course of action and was committed to it. She removed her foot from the brake pedal and jammed it onto the accelerator, causing the car to leap backwards.

Only then did she take her eyes off the man and turn her head in the direction the car had begun to travel. She fought the wheel to keep the careening vehicle from crashing into an embankment, trapping her and the child.

Her quick action was matched by the gunman. He raised the rifle and, with deliberate aim, started shooting into the fleeing vehicle.

The first bullet entered the car's windshield and passed through the front seat, inches from the woman's body. It continued its trajectory, through the rear seat of the car, through the trunk, and struck the highway.

If the bullet was intended to make her stop, it failed. Showered by glass particles from the windshield, and aware of the hole in the seat, Martha pressed harder on the accelerator.

A second bullet slammed into the radiator and was followed by a third which entered the hood, smashed through the glove compartment and shattered the glass bottle which Craig was still nursing. Slivers of glass, mixed with spilled milk, spewed over the infant and his mother. Another bullet found its way into the radiator of the car and a fifth damaged the ignition wires, causing the motor to miss, cough and almost die under the demand for more speed. Another bullet struck the radiator, splashing the remaining coolant onto the highway. Once again the man fired, the bullet exploding the car's battery.

But still Martha's frantic demand on the car's motor was being answered. The sputtering car moved backwards, erratically, over the highway, up a steep incline, widening the distance from the gunman who continued to fire. The last bullet struck the front bumper of the car and ricocheted onto the highway, screaming under the car and passing behind it.

Finally, the dying vehicle passed over the summit of the grade and out of the gunman's range.

Fear that the motor would quit if she attempted to stop the car and turn it around made Martha continue to nurse the engine in her reverse dash for safety. Added to her desperation was the sight of Craig, now bleeding from cuts on his face and hands, and crying hysterically from the pain.

Martha was unable to take her hands from the wheel long enough to stop Craig from rubbing his face, driving the splinters of glass further into his skin.

The sight of her sister's home brought Martha her first feeling of relief and security since the nightmare had begun. She released the wheel with one hand and started to pound the horn. Her sister ran to the steaming, smoking car just as the motor coughed for the last time.

Charles Yohn, the Cisney brothers and several other men were gathered at a small service station in Neelyton. At 7:30 P.M., Charles heard a rifle shot. "Probably someone shooting a groundhog," Yohn said to no one in particular. The shot seemed to come from the area of Dry Run Hollow along the Neelyton-Burnt Cabins Road. The echo had just dissipated when it was followed by another.

"No one around here can be that bad a shot," Wade Cisney said.

A silent count was made by the men and before the last crack died out one of them said, "That makes eight."

"Let's drive down that way and see what the guy was shooting at," Yohn said to Brady Cisney. It was obvious that whoever was doing the shooting was in for some friendly ribbing. Born to a life in which hunting was an integral part, they took pride in their sharpshooting ability.

They had driven about a mile and were near Dry Run Hollow when Wade Cisney stopped the car. "Well, I'll be damned, would you look at that!" he said. Directly in front of the car was a barricade of logs.

The three men removed the logs from the road and were about to re-enter the car when one of the men found an ejected shell from a .30 caliber rifle. "Whoever was doing the shooting must have been standing near here," he said.

A quick glance at the highway revealed two other ejected shells from the same gun. "Don't see a groundhog or anything else around here," Yohn added. "How about driving me down to Snyder's farm and I'll go along home with Martha?" he suggested. Cisney agreed, and the trio drove on.

When they arrived the Yohn car was parked in front of the farm house with the rear wheels partially on the highway. The shattered windshield stood out boldly against the angled rays of sunlight. The door on the driver's side was open.

Yohn's first thought was that his wife had wrecked the car. He jumped from the Cisney car before it came to a complete stop and ran to the house in search of his wife and child. He was followed closely by his friends.

In the kitchen doorway he saw his wife's tear-streaked face peering intently at her son stretched out on a table, crying from the pain of the cuts. "What happened?" Charles cried out.

"Oh, God," she said at seeing her husband and began to sob out her story.

Shock turned to anger and then rage as her account of the attack continued. "I'll get him," Yohn promised his wife. "We'll help you," the Cisney brothers echoed.

Martha notified their physician by telephone and was assured he would be at the farm within minutes. She was later given a sedative for her nerves and the baby was treated for minor cuts.

After Charles was certain that neither his wife nor his son was seriously injured, he borrowed a rifle from the Snyders and accompanied Earl Snyder and the Cisneys to the scene of the shooting. Before leaving, Yohn telephoned the state police at Huntingdon and reported the attack. The call was recorded at 8:00 P.M.

When Trooper Migatulski arrived at Dry Run Hollow at 8:30 P.M., a group of men was already searching the sides of the road. All were armed with rifles and shotguns.

Before joining the search party, the trooper radioed for assistance. In addition to a number of police officers, a large group of volunteer firemen from Orbisonia responded. The word spread rapidly and by 9:00 P.M. other men from Orbisonia, Shade Gap, Neelyton and Burnt Cabins joined in the hunt.

More than forty men gathered at Dry Run Hollow as it got darker. Several more discharged shells were found along the highway, but no tracks were located to indicate the direction the gunman had taken.

Later investigators ruled out the possibility of the gunman escaping in the direction of Neelyton, since Yohn and the Cisneys had moved along the highway immediately following the attack. The Snyders and Mrs. Yohn swore that no cars passed the farm in the direction of Burnt Cabins before the Cisney car arrived, further indicating that the gunman escaped on foot.

East and west remained as possible escape routes. An escape to the west would have taken the gunman over open fields, while an escape to the east could have been made undetected into the deep woods of the Neelyton Mountains of the Tuscarora Range.

The posse branched out at dawn on Thursday, this time to the wooded area leading to the foot of the mountains. The small stream where the Yohn car was first hit by the bullets was also searched thoroughly.

Under the circumstances, Martha Yohn was unable to give an accurate estimate of the gunman's height. "Standing there on the bank, he looked as big as a giant," she told the police.

Trooper Migatulski, in charge of the investigation, which was now getting intense, was taken off regular duty and assigned to the case on a full-time basis. Other officers were assigned to help him.

Eighteen "witnesses" were questioned in the ensuing investigation. Two "hard" suspects were picked up and taken to Huntingdon for questioning. Both were soon released after submitting to lie detector tests.

One of them was a man named William Hollenbaugh.

# MARY BLAKE *August 29, 1964*

Nearly two months had passed since the last attack by the Mountain Man, the nickname given to the gunman who made his escape into the Tuscaroras.

It was an unbelievable summer—hot and dry in the valley of Shade Gap, which was usually cool and green. Men, women and children were forced to live not knowing when the mountain man would attack again—or who would be his next victim.

Mary Blake, a twenty-one-year-old mother of two young children, paid Anne Weaver for some groceries and asked her to set the bags aside on the checkout counter. "I'll get the groceries as soon as I can get the children in the back seat," she told the woman, with whom she had become friendly.

But Anne Weaver had already pressed a buzzer on the checkout counter, summoning a boy to carry the groceries to the woman's car. "We'll take them out for you," she told Mary Blake. The youth came immediately. As they left the store, Anne Weaver noticed just how tiny Mrs. Blake was;

the school boy walking ahead of her towered over her five-foot stature.

She dismissed the thought as a man entered. Since the attack, Anne paid close attention to every male customer. She was looking for someone whose eyes were a vivid blue.

Mary Blake, who lived only two miles from the Hart Market, along the unpaved Mountain Foot road southwest of Shade Gap, arrived at her isolated frame home early in the afternoon. She let her children play in the yard while she prepared the evening meal.

Her husband, Harold, got home from work about 5:30 P.M. and the family sat down for supper. During the meal, the couple received word that Harold's mother was ill. Before leaving for his mother's, Harold reminded his wife to bring the children inside before dark and to make sure the doors of the house were locked. He loaded a rifle for his wife and placed it in the pantry.

Twilight came at 8:30 P.M. and Mary locked up the house for the night, then prepared the children for their bath. To busy herself, she ironed some clothes after the children were in bed. It was 10:50 P.M. when she heard the sound of an automobile approaching. She put down the iron and walked to the kitchen window, peering out into the night. The full moon was now behind clouds which had rolled in, promising a summer storm. She continued to look out of the window and with a flash of lightning, caught a fleeting glimpse of a 1956 model Chevrolet parked along the road. Instant and paralyzing fear came over her. She knew no one who drove a car of that make or model.

She did not see anyone move toward the house as she looked out. Normally a person would have walked past the window where she stood because the driveway was parallel to the side of the house. The front porch had been removed because it was no longer safe, leaving the rear door as the only entrance.

She waited only a moment at the window and was about to dismiss the incident as a lovers' tryst when she heard footsteps on the rear porch. The steps were followed by a knock at the door.

Mary walked quickly to the center of the kitchen and called out, "Who is it?" No one answered. She repeated the question loudly and started moving toward the pantry and the gun.

Whoever stood outside suddenly kicked the rear door, nearly forcing it open. Despite her fear, Mary was determined to protect herself and her children. As she wheeled around with the gun in her hands, another kick opened the door completely.

Facing her was a man attired in the regalia of a Halloween character—a grotesque orange and pink rubber mask, a faded green raincoat and galoshes. He was pointing a bolt action rifle held at belt level in her direction. "Put down the gun or I'll shoot you!" he ordered. Mary had already started to raise the weapon.

The Mountain Man fired his rifle and the bullet smashed into the stock of the gun she was holding. It then entered the woman's right hand at the knuckles and traveled into the flesh between her forefinger and thumb. Passing through her hand, the bullet exited above her wrist and penetrated the wall of the kitchen near the pantry.

The crack of the rifle rattled the windows in the small kitchen. The noise of the shooting, the thud of Mary's rifle striking the floor, and her cry of astonishment woke the children, who started to cry.

Oblivious to her pain, Mary stood fascinated as she looked at her right hand, now gushing blood. For a moment, the scene was frozen.

The gunman moved first, breaking the silence. "I told you to drop the gun. Why didn't you do what I said?" he asked, almost apologetically. Mary was riveted to the spot, swaying slightly as she stared at him with unbelieving eyes. He walked up to her and touched her gently on her wounded arm. Leading her to a chair at the kitchen table, he forced her to sit while he got a towel from the sink.

"I want you and a little wound like that isn't going to stop me," he said, wrapping her hand in a towel. Fully aware of his intention and her own defenselessness, she couldn't stop staring at this man who was about to attack her. The rubber mask covered his entire head and reached his shoulders. Its orange color contrasted with the green raincoat and black boots. But the greatest contrast of all were the outstanding eyes, giving a lifelike quality to the grotesque mask.

When the man was finished with the crude bandage, he stood up, picked up the rifle that had been propped against the table and said, "All right, let's get into the bedroom." No longer able to defy his orders, Mary stood up, swaying slightly on unsteady legs, and was helped by the gunman who took her arm in a viselike grip and walked slightly behind.

When the gunman reached around Mary and opened the bedroom door, the light from the kitchen silhouetted him in the doorway, causing the two children to cry again.

The gunman pushed Mary into the room, snarling, "Shut them kids up now, before I shut them up for you!" Still numb with fear, she crossed the floor to the crib, gathering them up. Her efforts were only slightly successful. "Be quiet now. Mommy is here with you," Mary soothed, then put them back to bed.

Then she turned and faced the gunman, "Please don't hurt them. They'll be quiet now," she said.

His harsh answer, "They'd better be quiet," only brought more cries from the crib.

"Damn," the gunman retorted, "we're getting the hell out of here." He grabbed Mary by the left arm and pulled her into the kitchen and toward the outside doorway.

"Don't make me go with you. I can't leave the children here alone," she pleaded.

Despite her attempts to hold back, the man propelled her towards the broken kitchen door. Rain was falling lightly as he forced her ahead of him into the night.

"You're going with me, and that's that," he said. He let go

of her arm and produced a flashlight from his raincoat pocket, shining it ahead of him in the direction of the woods.

She began to sob.

"Shut up and keep walking," he said as he flashed the light into a cornfield, now wet from the rain.

The cries of the children were becoming less audible as they walked between rows of waist-high corn.

Mary still felt no pain in her hand, but she suddenly realized that blood from the injury was saturating the makeshift bandage. She tried to stop, to explain that the bleeding was becoming severe, but her words made no sense. Her move only caused him to grip her arm tighter and propel her forcibly toward the woods.

"This is good enough, we'll stop here," he ordered as they reached the edge.

Mary sank onto the wet grass, sobbing. "I'm not the one you want. What did I ever do to you?" she asked in a pleading voice. The gunman stood over her.

"You've been wicked, and I'm going to make you pay for your sins," he told her. "Let me see your hand," he commanded, as he propped the rifle against the tree and directed the beam of the flashlight towards the wrapping.

Muttering an oath under the mask, the gunman said, "We're going to stop that bleeding before I get at you. Take off your pants," he ordered.

The sight of the blood-filled towel and a fear of dying made her follow his orders. She removed her pants with her left hand, holding her dress with the injured hand, which was now numb.

When she completed the uncomfortable task from her awkward position, the gunman took the panties from her and walked a short distance to a tree. There he broke off a small but strong branch and returned to the prostrate woman.

"Take the towel off your hand," he directed. "I'm gonna make a tourniquet with your pants and stop the bleeding." Her head bowed in shame, Mary followed his orders.

She almost fainted when she saw her shattered hand in

the glare of the flashlight. The wound was now exposed and started to bleed profusely. Quickly the man dropped to his knees and wrapped the underwear around her hand. He inserted the branch between the two leg holes, and twisted it until the bleeding stopped.

"Now hold onto the stick with your left hand, and if blood starts to run again, twist the stick harder," he commanded. He then raped her on the wet ground. The lightning, thunder and rain added to the unrealistic scene.

She cried quietly during the attack and was aware only of the sweaty odor of the man as he satisfied himself. Then she recognized his mutterings as passages from the Bible! "What kind of a twisted mind is this?" she wondered.

A wave of thoughts passed through her mind. Where was her husband? Suppose he was home and waiting for her now? How were the children? Would this monster now let her go? Who is he?

With the last thought, she reached for his mask and attempted to rip it off. The effort brought an immediate action. He slapped her weakened arm away and cursed her.

"You try that again and I'll kill you," he warned. "You'll never know who I am, so don't try another trick like that."

She knew then that if she could see him, she would know him. During flashes of lightning, she caught glimpses of his body. He was not wearing anything under the raincoat. His body seemed exceptionally hairy.

When he rose, he flashed the light onto her wounded hand and again uttered an oath. "You're bleeding again," he said in a voice which registered fear for the first time. "Tighten the stick so the bleeding will stop."

But twisting the stick a full turn failed to staunch the flow of blood which now stained the wet grass where she lay.

He buttoned his raincoat and helped her to her feet. Once she was standing, he pushed her ahead toward the house where she could see the light from the doorway.

When they were a short distance from the porch Mary heard the children crying inside the house. Free now, she ran toward the house and into the kitchen. She rushed into the bedroom, still holding tightly onto the makeshift tourniquet.

She had no sooner reached the side of the crib when she heard the sound of a motor. She ran to the bedroom window and stared out, hoping to get a glimpse of the escaping car. She saw what she thought to be the tail lights of a 1956 model Chevrolet.

Fully aware of the danger of bleeding to death, she chose to leave the safety of her home and her children and seek help. Blood dripped from her fingertips as she started out toward Shade Gap. She had made her way only a few hundred feet down the muddy road when headlights appeared over the rise.

It was Harold.

"Oh God, help me . . . I've been shot!" Mary called to her husband as he jumped from the car, leaving the motor running. She leaned heavily on the fender.

"What happened?" he asked in a voice choked with fear.

He took her wounded arm as panic hit the pit of his stomach. Gently he unwound the blood-smeared towel while she maintained a grip on the tourniquet.

"Christ Almighty, you're going to the hospital," he said in a shaking voice after seeing the gaping hole in his wife's wrist. "Get the children first, please," Mary begged in a flood of tears.

"Can you make it?" he asked as he quickly rewrapped her hand in the blood-soaked towel. She nodded. He helped his wife into the front seat and quickly drove home to the children.

"Jesus, it's quiet. What happened to the kids?" he wondered as he ran to the door. He had not heard a sound from the time he stopped the motor. He burst into the kitchen, and went straight to the bedroom. The children were asleep.

He was pulling the covers off the children when his wife made it to the bedroom door. "They're OK . . . thank God, they're OK," he repeated.

"Christ, what happened?" he asked again as he turned his

attention to his wife, propping herself up at the doorway.

"The Mountain Man shot me!" she gasped out. "He kicked in the door and shot me when I grabbed the rifle."

"The son of a bitch . . . the son of a bitch. I'll kill him. Who is he? What did he want? Did he do anything else to you? The bastard . . . he's dead, I tell you . . . he's just as good as dead right now," Harold screamed out in a rage. "Tell me on the way. You're going to the hospital right now. I'll get the kids bundled up in a blanket." In seconds he had both children in his arms as he ran past his wife to the car. "I'll be right back," he called as he moved through the kitchen door.

He returned and gently carried his wife to the car. He was about to enter it himself when he suddenly went back to the house. When he returned he had a rifle with him, checking to see that it was loaded.

Dirt and stones flew from the gravel as he jammed the vehicle out of the driveway and then toward Route 522 and the Fulton County Medical Center. Only after they reached the Medical Center did he take time to call the state police at Huntingdon.

By the time the investigators arrived, an ambulance was being readied to transport Mary to the Chambersburg Hospital. She was in no condition to be questioned and police were briefed by her husband.

Hours had now passed since the attack, and once again the Mountain Man had escaped, vanishing into the darkness as he had in the past.

Two state patrolmen from McConnellsburg's substation were dispatched to the Blake home. Long before daylight, more policemen arrived and went over every detail, some of it vague and second-hand from Harold Blake. Other officers were dispatched to the area to cordon off both vehicle and foot traffic in an effort to preserve clues.

Luck was on the side of the Mountain Man; the rain, which had come in torrents, destroyed all tracks in the muddy cornfield. Only through the trail of blood left behind by Mrs. Blake were officers able to track the path to the woods.

The slug from the .30 caliber rifle the Mountain Man had used was recovered. However, its passage through the woman's hand and wrist and entry into the kitchen wall had destroyed its ballistics value.

By daylight, word had traveled throughout the community. Every resident in the valley heard of the latest attack. Fear mounted again in the area, and new instructions to wives and children were given by men as they left their homes for work.

Then the tedious questioning began again. Did anyone hear anything? Did anyone have any idea who the man might be? Did anyone even have a suspicion? Neighbor looked at neighbor, friend at friend, relative at relative; and the doubts took over.

The timing of the Mountain Man's arrival at the Blake home was thought to be more than just coincidence. He had to be watching the home to take advantage of Harold's departure.

Alibis were checked. Men who were supposedly working had the embarrassment of an investigator's inquiry with their employer. Those who had the misfortune to be away from home that night had their private lives spread open publicly in the police spotlight. Yet despite the methodical and thorough search into everyone's life, police were just as baffled as before.

Mrs. Blake spent the next six weeks in a hospital after undergoing surgery. And though she regained partial use of her right hand, the emotional scars will always remain with her.

# NED PRICE   *April 16, 1965*

Good Friday brought the promise of an early summer. The sun was warm over the area, melting the last vestiges of snow in the mountaintops.

The dramatic change of season gave a false sense of security to the residents of Shade Gap Valley. With the exception of several minor peeping Tom reports and a few burglaries, the valley regained some of its peacefulness. It was almost eight months since Mary Blake had been shot and raped; still it was not a place to visit unannounced. Every homestead had a gun ready for immediate action. But most of the fear had disappeared with winter. Many even felt the Mountain Man had left the area.

Ned Price, a civilian railroad engineer at Letterkenny Army Depot, had thoughts only of the trout he would catch the next morning as he drove the thirty miles to his home, a mile and a half east of Shade Gap. At fifty-three, he was exceptionally active. He liked to hunt and fish, and, unlike many people in the neighborhood, had no fear of the Mountain Man. That the Mountain Man would choose as his next victim his wife, Jessie, several years younger and exceptionally attractive, was the last thought in his mind.

When Ned arrived home, Jessie told him she was going to take a bath before watching television. "I'm going out back to dig some fishing worms," he called as he walked out the door. She had already turned on the TV set and didn't hear him. As she undressed, she was totally unaware of the eyes watching her hungrily through the bathroom window. The bathroom faced dense woods and she never bothered to draw the blind.

Ned picked up an electric lantern and a bait can on the back porch. He grabbed his shovel and started moving around the side of the house. He walked less than twenty-five feet when he heard a noise. He swung the lantern in the same direction and saw a man wearing a trench coat and a peaked cap. He seemed about six feet tall and carried a rifle held across the front of his waist.

"Stop," Ned yelled. The single word had not been uttered when the gunman put the rifle to his shoulder and fired.

Price started to pitch forward before he realized he had been shot. As he toppled forward, the forefinger of his left hand snapped off the lantern, throwing the area into darkness.

Ned rolled over several times, the shovel and bait can tumbling down the steep terrace in front of him. As he came to rest, he heard his attacker scramble up the thirty-foot-high embankment behind the property.

Ned tried to rush back into his home for a gun. He realized he had been seriously injured when he attempted to stand and use his left leg. The leg, with boot and trouser attached, dangled at a crazy angle midway between the ankle and knee.

"Jessie, help," he screamed. There was no response, only the muted sound of the television. Ned started to crawl along the embankment toward the kitchen. He looked back at the lower portion of his leg, amazed at its odd angle.

Dragging himself across the cindered driveway onto the porch, he pounded on the kitchen door. "Where the hell is she . . . she must hear me by now," he thought.

Jessie had finished bathing and was sprawled across the davenport in the living room when she heard the pounding on the door. At first, she thought a friend had come to visit and went into the kitchen to look. She screamed when she saw the door swing open with her husband's hand on the door knob, struggling to get inside the house.

"Pull me in . . . I've been shot," Ned yelled again as the door swung open and slammed against the wall.

Fear shot through her as she rushed to Ned and tugged at his shoulders. Blood smeared the floor.

"Shut the door quickly . . . the bastard may still be out there," Ned yelled over a second scream from his wife.

She tried, but couldn't close it completely. The shattered leg blocked the door. "Pull it in . . . pull it in," Ned urged as she stood horrified at the sight.

She touched the blood-covered boot and screamed again when it tumbled grotesquely out of the way of the door.

"Make a tourniquet out of something. Here, take my belt," he said when she failed to respond. He ripped off the belt and slipped it under his leg and told Jessie to draw it as tight as she could. "Tighter . . . tighter," he said. They both watched the blood slow to a trickle.

He helped her pull the belt tighter and held it with both hands. She threw a towel beside him on the floor and he twisted it into a second tourniquet.

"Call my brother. Get him up here as quickly as possible. Then call an ambulance. The bastard must have shot my leg the whole way off," Ned said through a grimace of pain.

She didn't want to leave her husband, yet she didn't want to stay in the kitchen and watch him bleed. Another command brought her back to reality and she rushed into the living room to make the urgent calls. Fortunately there was no one on the party line and Ned's brother, Guy, answered immediately.

Before Guy arrived Jessie placed a call to Dr. George

Baumgardner at Orbisonia. As he left his office, he placed a call for an ambulance.

When Guy burst through the back door, he stepped in his brother's blood, which was now covering most of the kitchen floor. Between curses, he asked what happened. When told it was the Mountain Man, he cursed again and threatened to kill him.

Within an hour Troopers Dick Fischer and Bob Kissner had pulled into the Prices' yard. Greeting them was the scene of a minor disaster: flashing lights from an ambulance, cars parked half on the highway, and a growing crowd of people moving about. Other vehicles, attracted by the siren and the speeding cruiser, had fallen in line and were pulling up as the officers walked toward the house.

The troopers stepped onto the porch as the ambulance attendants carried Price through the kitchen door. Price looked at Kissner, and through clenched teeth said, "Out back." Jessie, still wearing a housecoat, was trying vainly to walk with the stretcher, her tear-stained face showing the impact of the event.

Dr. Baumgardner, following the stretcher, took Kissner's arm and propelled him toward the ambulance. "He's in bad shape . . . no way can we save the leg. If it hadn't been for the tourniquet . . ." he left the obvious conclusion unspoken. The ambulance door was closed behind the physician and his patient and the vehicle sped away.

Kissner took Jessie's arm and led her back to the house. Fischer, in the meantime, stood in the driveway, midway between the house and road, and directed the growing crowd of curiosity seekers away from the scene before they destroyed any clues.

It was then that Trooper Ruegg arrived and assumed the responsibility of the investigation. He directed Kissner to radio for help, and helped Fischer keep people away from the area.

"Get some bloodhounds in here. We can track the bastard

while the trail is still hot," Kissner directed. Additional police were en route by the time Ruegg began questioning Guy and Jessie.

Even in the dark it was easy to see where the attack took place. Price had left behind an unmistakable trail of blood.

Within an hour a dozen policemen were on the scene. Mrs. Price was driven to the Huntingdon Hospital to join her husband, and a bloodhound was brought in from Carlisle. A careful search of the area revealed where the gunman stood when he shot Price. The spent shell of the high-powered rifle was found in the wet grass.

The bathroom window revealed the reason for the nightly visits by the phantom—a clear view of the interior. Other evidence indicated the visitor had made repeated visits. Discarded candy bar and chewing gum wrappers were found beneath the window, and semen had been ejaculated onto the wall. From the window, a well-defined path led into the dense wood behind the home.

Tom Stewart, along with his veteran bloodhound, arrived at the Price home shortly after 11:00 P.M. He led the dog to the bathroom window where the intruder had stood only hours before. The animal picked up the scent immediately and announced the accomplishment with its unique bark.

Troopers Ruegg and Migatulski, along with six fellow officers and nearly a dozen relatives and friends of the Prices, scaled the thirty-foot embankment at the rear of the home and began the cross-country manhunt. Everyone was armed. The trail reached a dead end at a little-used mountain road. The dog stopped barking. Despite all efforts of the trainer to help his animal onto a new track, the bloodhound was stymied. The search party was forced to admire the elusiveness of their adversary.

The shooting of Price made it clear he would stop at nothing if surprised or cornered. He would do as his insane drive compelled, and damn the consequences.

The description of the man given by Price added to the confusion of the identity of the gunman. He could have been anyone in the valley. The victims to date had described him as young, middle-aged, and old. He was further described as being short, medium and tall. He was slim, well built and heavy. And with the exception of his eyes, no description was yet made of his face or hair. He either wore a mask or his face was not seen.

No one in the valley, especially the police, believed he was finished. He would return.

The crowd of onlookers at the Price home grew during the absence of the posse. State Police Detective Al Broscius, Harrisburg, was now in charge of the investigation. He had roped off the area and was waiting for daylight, when the area would be extensively searched.

In the meantime, roadblocks were set up throughout the valley. Every moving vehicle was stopped and searched, and the occupants questioned. If trailers were sealed and the seal was intact, the cabs were searched. If not, the entire rig was given a thorough once-over.

All information gathered in the night was compiled and added to the volumes of material made available since the first attack on Mrs. Jacka. It all added up to nothing!

By morning, specially trained crews of investigators were at the Price home and the ejected shell of the gun was carefully studied. It was found to be nothing more than a twisted piece of metal, identifiable only by caliber. All tracings of the slug were gone, ripped away by the flesh, bone, wood and asphalt.

There were no identifiable footprints found in the area under the window. All other footprints had been obliterated by the posse.

Dr. Baumgardner returned by mid-Saturday morning with the news that Price would pull through, but that an emergency operation had been performed during the night to amputate the lower part of his leg.

For the next months, the police were zealous in their attempts to capture the Mountain Man. Suspects were followed and checked out: a gas station operator opening up early one morning; a farmer milking his cows; even a man out on the road very early one Sunday to pick up newspapers for his son's paper route.

The investigation was not successful. The residents of the area were hostile to the policemen and not over-anxious to tell them anything. They preferred giving clues and news to local reporters.

Dozens of men were taken to Huntingdon to face a lie detector. One, a school bus driver, lost his job as a result of the questioning. Although he was cleared by the police, school children refused to board his bus, still fearing he might be guilty. His wife received ominous phone calls; he was unemployed—and the Mountain Man was still at large.

The investigators kept at it, searching the area behind the Price house for new evidence. Yet nothing showed up. But as long as the gunman remained free, the residents kept up their self-imposed barriers. While their men were at work, women gathered at each other's houses or stayed behind closed doors. Husbands took their wives to work with them. Neighbors exchanged views on self-defense. Hitchhikers were warned to steer clear of the area; motorists were advised to keep moving. It was no place to have a flat tire—or to run out of gas.

### APRIL 1966
"He's still here . . . I know it and I can feel it."
—Ned Price

One year ago, Ned Price had his leg shot off. Two years ago, Viola Jacka, Anne Weaver, Mary Blake, Martha Yohn all had been victims of the Mountain Man. Yet, officials in the area were no closer to finding the phantom gunman than they had been in April, 1964.

The raids by the Mountain Man had taken their toll: neighbor mistrusted neighbor, friend turned against friend. The children of the area had a new game—Kill the Sniper. Mothers kept watchful eyes on their children. Where once they were allowed to play freely, they were now restricted to fenced-in yards.

And what of the people whose lives had been directly touched by the mysterious sniper? Viola Jacka abandoned her house and moved in with relatives. Mary Blake and family moved out of the area and in with her parents. Martha Yohn kept a loaded pistol with her at all times. Anne Weaver left her home for a year and a half, then moved back. She still refused to spend the night alone at her house, and bought a dog for protection and companionship. Ned Price was fitted with an artificial limb. He and Jessie sold their house and bought a mobile home, near the old house, but closer to the highway and within sight of neighbors.

And the residents of the area turned to the local news media. Distrusting the law enforcement officers, possibly because the case was still unsolved, they turned to Bob Cox as friend, confidant, intermediary. Any clues, any hints, any new developments, were relayed by the frightened people of Shade Gap to Cox. He, in turn, would contact the police with whatever information he had.

But this was no way to live. The Shade Gap area was silent, but as one resident said, "It was a deafening silence."

# JOAN McMICHAEL   *May 5, 1966*

It was getting dark. Luther McMichael was preparing to take the family car to a garage in the Shade Gap area, a mile away, for repairs. Even though it had been over a year since the Mountain Man's attack on Ned Price, McMichael warned his young wife: "Stay inside. Don't answer the door for anyone you don't recognize. And make sure the doors are locked as soon as I leave."

"Don't worry, I'll be all right. Just come home as soon as possible," she urged.

The McMichaels had moved to the Shade Gap area with their two sons, an infant and an eighteen-month-old toddler, only two months ago, after Joan was forced to quit work in a dress factory at Warfordsburg. The less expensive living quarters were within the family budget, but under their newly adopted austerity, they couldn't afford a telephone.

Although she had relatives in the area, she didn't put as much belief in the Mountain Man as did the residents who had lived there for the past two years.

Joan started washing the dishes after cleaning off the

supper table, talking to her children as she worked. The infant, in a playpen in the kitchen, was playing with a rattle, content with the closeness of his mother and the bright lights and noise. Luther, Jr., was playing with an empty catsup bottle and a tin can. "Don't do that, Luther. You'll break the bottle," she repeated when the youngster struck the bottle against the can for the umpteenth time. In a fit of anger, the child tossed the catsup bottle toward his baby brother and it spun across the floor under the playpen.

"That did it," Joan snapped while reaching for a dry towel. "Out it goes," she scolded.

Without giving the safety of her home a second thought, she gathered up the bottle and can. "And you will just go along with me to see where these things go, then you won't have to look for them again," she chided, picking Luther up with her free hand and bracing his weight on her hip.

When she reached the kitchen door and found it locked, she realized she shouldn't be going outside. She glanced to her left out the kitchen window and saw that it was not totally dark and thought, "I can't back out now. If I don't throw these things away, I'll have no peace the rest of the night."

She unlocked the door, took a final look at her younger child, still playing blissfully, and opened the door. It was light enough so she could see to the edge of the porch where she would drop the articles into the open trash can.

With Luther balanced on her hip, her hand released the bottle and can without direction. She was gazing to the west, almost directly to her right, when a cold strong hand wrapped itself around her right ankle from below the elevated porch.

Joan screamed and jerked her leg free from the grip, looking down at the same time. A man with a long dark stocking pulled over his head started to stand up. Almost frozen to the spot, she stared at the grotesque apparition rising to its full height. He wore a long dark coat, her mind recorded. And the holes slit in the stocking were so small she could not see the eyes.

Then reality set in. Facing her was the man who had already crippled two and caused fear and distrust in hundreds of others.

She screamed again, whirled around, and ran across the porch to the open kitchen door. Every step of the way she expected to be grabbed again or worse, shot in her tracks. The fifteen feet of wooden floor beneath her feet seemed endless.

Without turning around, she slammed the heavy door behind her and twisted the key in the lock. She dropped Luther on legs that had only recently mastered walking and ran to the kitchen window. She glanced at the center sash, saw it was locked and pulled down the shade.

"You stay here, don't do anything," she said to Luther, Jr. "I'm going to make sure all the doors and windows are locked."

She left the kitchen and made a furious check of the rest of the doors and windows on the first floor. Back in the kitchen, she glanced at the wall clock and saw that it was just 8:30 P.M., only ten minutes since her husband had left. The old house was well built, but anyone could smash a window or kick down a door and the man she saw outside only minutes ago had seemed big enough to smash down a wall. She and her children were trapped, locked inside a prison with no means of contacting help. Her husband was only a mile away, but he might as well have been on the moon. She was alone and her only hope was that the man outside didn't know it.

Regaining some of her composure, she began to soothe the children, and at the same time to get control of her own emotions.

She took a wooden chair and placed it against the door, under the knob, for what little added protection it gave. She returned to the playpen and lifted Luther into it with his younger brother, urging both to go to sleep. She stayed by their side on her knees, turning her face away as she began to weep.

Thirty minutes later, she rose on stiff legs, her eyes now

dry, and walked to the kitchen sink. From the drawer, she took out her largest kitchen knife, then returned to her sons.

This time she sat on the floor beside the sleeping boys. Her mind recorded nearly every minute her husband was gone . . . thirty, forty-five, sixty.

She had cried herself out when the clock reached 10:30 P.M. Now she was afraid for her husband.

She was satisfied that she and her children were safe. If the madman had wanted to, he would have broken down the door by this time. Oddly, she now remembered that she hadn't heard a sound for the last two hours.

Suppose he was waiting outside for Luther to return, to shoot him when he stepped from the car? He would then have the rest of the night to break in without fear of being stopped by anyone.

Holding her breath, she crawled to the kitchen door and pressed her ear against the cold surface, trying to catch a sound from outside. Only the noise of cars and trucks passing on the nearby highway could be heard.

The night dragged on. It was 11:30 P.M. when she heard a car shifting gears and drawing closer. All the fears she had been repressing swelled now, when she realized the car was Luther's. He would stop the car, get out and get shot. Then she noticed that she still held the butcher's knife. The madman would have to kill us both then, she thought to herself.

She stood by the kitchen door and when the car stopped in the driveway, she unlocked the door and shouted, "Luther, the Mountain Man is out there. Watch yourself."

She ran across the porch, jumped down the steps toward her husband, yelling as she ran. A shocked Luther grabbed his wife's arm, which held the knife at a threatening angle, and was nearly knocked over when her body slammed into his.

"What the hell are you talking about? What's going on here?"he asked.

"The Mountain Man, he was here. He grabbed me by the leg," she was screaming and started to cry again.

"My God," was his only response as he moved his head from side to side, peering into the darkness near the home.

"Let's get inside. Run!" he yelled to Joan. They ran, hand in hand, up the porch steps and through the open door into the lighted kitchen. Both boys were awakened by the noise and began to cry.

In the safety of the kitchen, with the door locked behind them, Joan unfolded the story as it had happened. Meanwhile, Luther secured his rifle and loaded it.

Fearing that the intruder could still be outside, they did not notify the police until daybreak. Then Luther, Joan and the two children, exhausted from maintaining the nightlong vigil, drove to a relative's home and telephoned the Huntingdon substation.

Ned Price had told friends the previous day the Mountain Man was going to come out of hiding again. Even he would have doubted that the prophecy would be fulfilled so soon.

And it was only beginning. . . .

# MARY LOU
# BRODERICK

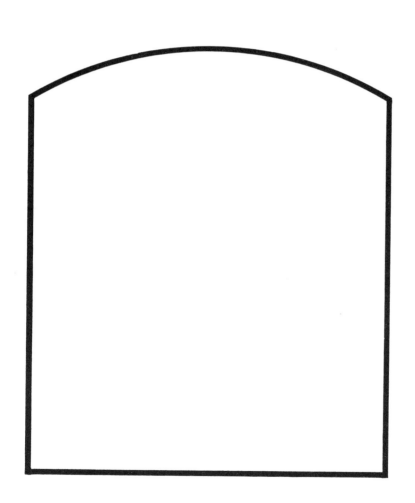

# THE FIRST DAY     *Wednesday, May 11, 1966*

Mary Lou Broderick wasn't thinking of the bus ride home. The 3:25 bell had sounded the end of another school day and she was looking for several of her girl friends. She would make tentative plans for another Saturday trip to the Blue Mountain Roller Rink at Roxbury.

Mary, a seventeen-year-old junior in high school, enjoyed skating. She was pretty and fully developed, and the rink was always filled with her friends.

The weekend would be fun, she thought, as she pulled a jacket over her red corduroy jumper and white blouse. Weekends made school bearable, especially since there was less than a month to go.

When the final bell rang, the mad dash for the exits began. The "see you tomorrows" were bantered about and the long row of yellow parked buses in the student loading area filled quickly.

Mary sat beside a window near the rear. She would be one of the last off the bus driven by Isaac Frehn of Shade Gap. She sat directly behind her brother, Joe, sixteen, also a high school student, and the other Broderick children who were already on the bus when it pulled into the high school lot—Alice Beth, eleven; Karen Lee, eight; Jane Ellen, nine; and Jane's twin brother, Dan Lester.

"It could rain before the night's over," she thought to herself glancing out of the window. As she checked her wrist watch it was just a couple of minutes before 4:00 P.M. The bus rounded a curve and now she could see her grandmother's house at the side of the road. She sometimes got off here and spent a little time before going home, but decided to pass up the visit today. The bus moved on. A short time later it came to a stop at the end of the dirt road. It was 4:00 P.M. when Frehn flipped on the four-way blinkers and opened the door for the six to alight.

The children walked leisurely up the slight incline toward their home, a half-mile ahead. From a grove of trees a man appeared and walked toward them. He looked like a hunter, a common sight in the mountain area. A gun hung over his shoulder.

The children showed some interest in him, but it was nothing more than curiosity. The path the man was taking, however, put him on an intersecting course with the children. The children's interest grew as he drew nearer.

Mary was especially curious, wondering who the man could be. She couldn't get a clear look at his face. He was looking down as he approached, almost as if he were picking each step.

Mary, who was walking slightly ahead of her brothers and sisters, was ready to offer an acknowledgment of friendship to the stranger when he took the gun from his shoulder and pointed it toward the children. He raised his eyes from the road and the children saw why he had kept his head down. He was wearing dark glasses over a black eye mask, effectively disguising his appearance.

"I don't want any sass out of you," he commanded in a deep and rough-sounding voice. The children stopped in their tracks.

Mary blurted, "What do you—" but she never got a chance to finish the sentence.

"You, I want you. You're coming with me, right now," he commanded and grabbed Mary by the left arm, keeping the gun aimed at the other children. Joe made an involuntary movement toward his sister and the man, who whirled her toward the little group in front of him.

"Don't do it," he commanded and moved the barrel of the gun in a direct line to Joe. Joe stopped cold.

"Please, you don't—" Mary started to say.

"Shut up and start moving," the man said, directing her toward the opposite side of the road. He shoved her forward, her 119-pound, 5-foot, 4-inch frame literally jerked from its spot. The books she carried fell, and loose papers scattered over the road.

An automatic movement to stop and retrieve her things brought a sharp response from the man. "Let them go, you won't be needing them anymore." His vise-like grip on her arm did not relax as the pair stopped a few feet from the road, standing in a tangle of greenbrier.

Mary, sobbing, glanced helplessly back to her sisters and brothers. A slight movement toward them brought only a tightening of the vise. She cried out and was spun away from her siblings by the powerful man.

"Now go—run," he ordered again in a rough voice. The two moved off in a trot, eastward toward a wooded area.

The children watched helplessly as their sister disappeared in the woods. Then realization set in and pandemonium followed. They started to scream, yell, cry and run toward home.

"He's got Mary . . . Oh my God . . . he's kidnapped her . . . Mary, come back, don't go," the children screamed. Karen and Jane stopped to pick up two books before joining the rest of the children.

Joe, with strong legs pumping mechanically, covered the distance in a minute, with the others trying vainly to keep up. All were yelling and crying as they approached home, but it was Joe who burst through the front door, calling to his father.

"He's got Mary . . . the Mountain Man's got Mary. He took her into the woods," he yelled when he saw his father sitting in the kitchen. "He held us up with a gun and took Mary," Joe gasped.

George Broderick jumped up. His face was colorless as he swore, "The son-of-a-bitch . . . the son-of-a-bitch." He reached out, grabbed the readied shotgun propped against the kitchen wall and said, "Come on," to his son. They ran out the door and almost ran into the four children who had just gotten home.

"Stay here. Go in the house," the father commanded the youngsters as he and Joe ran toward the car. Stones and dirt flew from beneath the rear wheels as George jammed the accelerator to the floor, letting out the clutch in a single motion. Jerking the wheel hard, to keep from spinning out of control, he aimed it toward the bus stop. Broderick pressed the horn of the car tightly, hoping to frighten off the kidnapper.

Mute evidence of the abduction greeted his eyes when he reached the spot where the girl disappeared. The movement of the car spun loose papers into the air again. But there was nothing else. His daughter and her kidnapper had vanished.

"Mary, Mary," he called.

No answer.

Father and son exchanged hopeless glances, then bolted across the empty field in pursuit. Both called out "Mary," as they ran side by side.

There was no response to their pleading calls. They ignored the slap of the low-hanging branches on their faces, the tearing of their trousers, and the scratches on their legs, as they ran through the underbrush.

When the pair were about a half-mile into the woods, they suddenly stopped the chase. "It's useless. We'll have to get help. We'll have to call the police," Broderick told his son between gasps for breath. Joe nodded.

They traced their steps through the woods again, running as fast as they could. Reaching the car, they headed toward the nearest telephone, the home of Constable Eugene Frank Clippinger, not far away.

Clippinger, an employee of the Pennsylvania Glass and Sand Company, Mapleton Depot, and a part-time school bus driver, heard the squeal of the tires and the roaring of the motor long before he saw the Broderick car. He jerked open his front door just as George and Joe jumped from the car.

"The Mountain Man's got Mary. I've got to use your phone to call the police," George hollered out as he approached the front porch.

"My God, when, where did it happen?" Clippinger asked, not expecting an answer as he continued, "I'll place the call. I know the number."

"Just up at the bus stop, just a few minutes ago. They've gone. They disappeared into thin air just like that," Broderick answered with a snap of his fingers. "Joe and I tracked them to the stream in the woods and then lost them. They can't be far away, they're just across the fields there," he continued, pointing out the front door of the Clippinger home north to the wooded area.

Clippinger completed the call and handed the phone to George. "Hello, this is the Huntingdon County State Police," an officer answered. "Can I help you?"

"My daughter was kidnapped. She was kidnapped just after she got off the bus. The Mountain Man has her. Get down here fast," Broderick was shouting into the telephone.

"Whoa, there, back up a minute. Get hold of yourself and start again. Who are you, and what is your daughter's name?" the officer asked.

"Oh, damn it, this is George Broderick in Shade Gap. That S.O.B. has taken my daughter, Mary, into the mountains down here," George said into the telephone.

"OK, OK, now hold on a minute. Let me connect you to Officer Ruegg. He's in charge of the investigation there," the officer said. Without waiting for an answer from Broderick, he turned and called for one of his fellow officers to get Ruegg. The message could be heard in the background by Broderick, who was near desperation. He had turned with the telephone in his hand, and was looking towards the woods where his daughter disappeared when Ruegg was connected. Broderick repeated who he was, where he lived and that his daughter had been kidnapped. "We'll be right there. Now hold on and give the officer the complete details. Where are you now?" he asked.

Broderick replied, "At the home of the constable."

Ruegg responded, "I know where that is. Stay put and I'll meet you there." He handed the telephone back to the duty officer.

"Start from the beginning, Mr. Broderick. Give me everything you have, every detail. The men are on their way so don't worry. We'll get your daughter back safely." The officer spoke in a tone designed to calm the distraught father.

"Hell, I really don't know anything. Let me put my son, Joe, on and he can give you the details. He was with Mary when the bastard kidnapped her," Broderick said.

In another room of the police barracks, Trooper Ruegg placed a call to district headquarters at Hollidaysburg, to forward the kidnapping message that he had just received. Captain Edward Swatij, commander of Troop G, told Ruegg to take another officer and move out to the scene immediately. He would dispatch Lieutenant Edward Mitarnowski and other offices to take charge of the search.

Joe took the telephone from his father's trembling hand and identified himself to the officer at Huntingdon. After a description of Mary was given, including the clothing she wore, the young man described the abduction. His voice broke under the tension.

"That's fine, young man," the officer said. "I've got it all now. Please put your father back on the telephone and don't worry. We'll get your sister back safely," he assured Joe.

"Lemme tell you something funny," Broderick said into the telephone. "I grabbed my shotgun when Joe and I took off after the son-of-a-bitch. Guess what? It wasn't even loaded."

At 4:30 P.M., Ruegg, accompanied by Trooper John Laskey, sped out of the barracks in Huntingdon, en route to Shade Gap, twenty-five miles to the south. Barely an hour had passed since Mary Lou Broderick had boarded the school bus. Ruegg had made the same trip to the Dublin Township community so many times he could have driven it blindfolded.

It had been his home-away-from-home for the past two years, but he was certain now his assignment would come to an end. A kidnapping, and in broad daylight, is an act of desperation, he thought, and a desperate man is not only dangerous; he is careless.

Joe Broderick had given the duty officer a description of the kidnapper, and Ruegg kept thinking about it. He tried to find a connection in the thoughts he had compiled in the investigation. Who was the kidnapper? Who was five feet, eight or nine inches tall, with a slim build and badly decayed front teeth? Was the kidnapper really the Mountain Man?

He mentally matched up the physical description with the apparel described by Joe: gray clothing, gray coat, knee-high boots and an orange-colored cap. That damned baseball cap again. And a mask under dark glasses yet. It was too much for his concentration now. He would wait until he got there and could review everything with the Brodericks.

Meanwhile, the telephones were all busy in Shade Gap. George Broderick called his wife's employer, who promised to take her home immediately. Then Clippinger took over the telephone and began firing out the news to men he knew would be available to help. They in turn called other people. Within minutes, the valley was mobilized. Men rushed to Clippinger's home armed with every type of weapon. They arrived on motorcycles, in cars, on bicycles and in trucks. They wore hunting clothes, in preparation for the search they knew would take them into the mountains. Each greeted Broderick with a promise of assistance, with their lives if necessary. All were genuinely saddened for the unemployed man, but secretly grateful it wasn't one of their own children.

One of the first to arrive on the scene was Isaac Frehn, who got the word of the kidnapping shortly after his bus run. Another was Ned Price.

As the crowd in the front of the constable's home swelled, other familiar faces showed up, including Charles Yohn. These men, above all others, had a personal interest. They had been touched by the madman and wanted to get even.

At 5:00 P.M., only fifty-five minutes since Mary had been kidnapped, Ruegg's police cruiser stopped at the constable's home. The two officers were met by Broderick and were immediately directed to the scene of the kidnapping.

Within a couple of minutes after the arrival of the officers, Trooper Laskey and fifteen armed volunteers set out in pursuit of the kidnapper. Ruegg stayed behind at the cruiser, gathering more information from Joe. He then placed a radio call to Huntingdon requesting a bloodhound. There were still almost two hours of daylight left and the posse led by Broderick was making good time as it disappeared into the woods.

Other cruisers from Huntingdon and McConnellsburg were being dispatched to the scene, directed to take different routes and search for the kidnapper and Mary. State police from Chambersburg, thirty-five miles away, were put on alert, and those already on the road were directed to stop all traffic at the Franklin County line.

At 5:05 P.M., Sergeant William Kimmel, in charge of the Huntingdon substation, learned of a helicopter operating in the area for the Department of Forests and Waters. After receiving clearance from troop headquarters, Sergeant Kimmel contacted the pilot and directed him to fly to the scene of the kidnapping.

The chopper skimmed the treetops of the valley, east of

the abduction scene, to the summit of the towering Tuscarora Mountains.

Troopers Sam Kline and Ronnie Weigand, patrolling north of Chambersburg, were aware of the kidnapping and attempted to follow the search on the shortwave radio. "Here we go," they said in unison as they picked up the message that additional troopers in the area were requested. Both had been expecting it and had actually been driving in the general direction of the incident.

Kline turned down the volume of the shortwave just as the Chambersburg state police blared out a message to their cruiser. "Proceed to the top of Neelyton Mountain and put a roadblock into effect. Stop all traffic going in and search all traffic before it leaves. You'll be relieved later and then proceed to Shade Gap," the message concluded.

"Kick in the afterburner," Kline told Weigand after he identified the car by number and gave a terse "ten-four."

"Jeez, everybody who works at the Letterkenny Army Depot can't live in Shade Gap," Weigand bitched as he wove in and out of the traffic heading west toward Timmons Mountain.

Trailing the cruiser were dozens of vehicles that had hugged the side of the road when the police car passed. None of the people knew why the police cruiser sped by. Most thought a serious accident lay ahead, and that the police were anxious to reach the scene.

The cruiser had blocked both lanes of traffic by the time the first trailing car reached the summit. Cars backed up a half-mile while the officers questioned each driver before allowing him to pass. Permission to move was given only after each was ordered not to stop along the way and not to pick up any hitchhikers. The only information given out by the officers was a straight "There has been a kidnapping," and nothing else.

The scene was one of war with an unknown enemy. It was a thousand against one, but the adversary was in command. He was still the Mountain Man, the specter who for two years appeared and disappeared at will.

There was a new determination in the valley, a will that

was born out of the brutality of the act. It not only marked the faces of men and women who were natives of the glen, but registered in the expressions of police.

At 6:30 P.M., Troopers Weigand and Kline were split up—Weigand because he was an assigned driver of the cruiser, and Kline because he knew the area. Two police cars from Carlisle had to be dispatched to the summit of the mountain to relieve the Chambersburg men.

Kline rode shotgun with another trooper not familiar with the valley. Weigand was accompanied by an officer who had been in the area on other occasions.

Overcast clouds brought an early twilight and the threat of rain as Kline directed his new partner to the scene of the abduction.

Turning off Route 641 at the old schoolhouse, Kline realized who the victim was. He had been at the Broderick home only two weeks before, looking to buy it for a hunting cabin. The "For Sale" sign was still in view when the cruiser arrived. The house was now a scene of bustling activity as newsmen from the area set up shop.

Kline saw two familiar faces—Bob Cox and Ken Peiffer—whom he had permitted to pass through the roadblock atop the mountain. "Get it solved yet, snoops?" he asked the newsmen when they approached his vehicle.

"Hell, yes, had it figured out an hour ago but I'm gonna let you jokers sweat. Wanna make this a really big story," Cox replied.

As the cruiser moved on to the spot where the kidnapping took place, the second search for Mary Lou and her abductor started. It was 6:30 P.M. and getting dark.

A half-dozen police, most in uniform, led twenty local residents into the woods, taking the same path as the first search party. Kline heard a remark from a passing member of the posse: "Jest let me get the son-of-a-bitch in my sights, that's all I want."

Kline remarked to his driver, "Christ, I'd hate to be a hunter coming home across the fields."

At 6:30 P.M., George Broderick, weary from the several

cross-country chases, was driven to nis home. His wife had been placed under the care of a physician.

A tearful reunion was held in the bedroom. The physician and the investigators stepped onto the front porch to allow a few short minutes of privacy to the grieving family. The officials passed on what little information was available to the crowd, now numbering in the dozens—newspapermen, radiomen and the curious. Television crews were on the way to spread their version of the kidnapping to the world.

There was no clue to the identity of the kidnapper, no clue to the whereabouts of the victim, no sightings by the helicopter or any of the police and volunteers in the hunts. There were now forty policemen on duty in the area, and more than twice that number of volunteers.

Police officials reported there would be other searches made within an hour and newsmen were invited to go along. There were also other orders: stay out of remote areas and quit tailing police cruisers.

The picture unfolding now was the biggest manhunt in the history of Pennsylvania. It covered forty square miles of the roughest terrain in the state, and could branch out quickly.

Police were not overlooking flight by car. Roadblocks, both east and west of the valley, were set up not only on all primary and secondary roads, but on the Turnpike as well.

In addition to the mobilization of all men of troop headquarters, police were rushing into the valley from Harrisburg, Chambersburg, Hanover, Lewistown, McConnellsburg, Carlisle and Gettysburg. Peace officers from other cities in the widespread area were also arriving by the carload, offering their help.

State foresters, game protectors, constables and deputy sheriffs from sixty miles away were converging on the scene. Radio stations, normally operating on a dawn-to-dusk FCC authorization, were granted permission to remain on the air to pass along progress of the investigation.

Weigand, after dropping off his new partner along Alternate 522 at the base of Neelyton Mountain, picked up a man who had spent a lifetime in the valley. The two were directed to search all side roads and abandoned buildings. Weigand's former rider had been assigned to stay with twelve local residents along the Dry Run Hollow Road.

"Just call me Charlie," the Shade Gap man said. He opened the door of the cruiser, pushed the business end of a double-barreled shotgun in the front of the car under Weigand's nose and plunked down beside the officer.

"Ronnie Weigand—call me Ron," the officer said as he leaned back on the seat to get his head out of the sights of the gun. "That thing loaded?" the officer asked, showing a row of teeth that he hoped to keep a bit longer.

"Yep. And it don't take much to set 'Bessie' off," Charlie answered with obvious pride. Hurt showed on Charlie's face when Weigand told him to unload the gun and put it in the back seat.

Weigand put the car in gear and asked, "Where to?"

"Just go down here a ways, past Decorum. There's an abandoned sawmill back off the road," Charlie directed. "The son-of-a-bitch could be holed up there," he added, caressing a handgun that was to be his companion for the rest of the night.

Several minutes of driving brought the cruiser to a dirt road, leading into the mountains south of where Mary Lou was kidnapped. Charlie directed, "Turn in here. It's back thataway a piece." He pointed into the darkened woods.

"OK. Can we make it back there?" the officer asked. "Looks like the ruts are kinda deep."

"Nothin' to it. Everybody travels these back roads, hereabouts," Charlie replied. Weigand gave a doubtful grunt.

The cruiser, geared for speed, shuddered as it moved slowly up the hill. Low-hanging branches swished against the side of the vehicle, swatted the red flasher on the roof and slapped the men's faces.

With the lights of the cruiser penetrating the darkness, shadows moved behind trees and brush, arousing the adrenalin in policeman and woodsman alike. The mile from the paved road seemed like fifty, as the car's headlights located the sawmill.

With the headlights still on, Weigand snapped off his seatbelt and took out his service revolver. Charlie was balancing his automatic in his hand when they separated to opposite sides of the sawmill.

"Mary," Weigand called out, as he made his way around the left side. "Mary," Charlie echoed from the other side of the time-blackened wooden discards. No answer.

"Didn't see anything my way. How'd you make out?" Charlie asked.

"Me neither. Don't look like anybody's been up here for years—maybe never," Weigand responded.

Weigand pulled the cruiser around in the clearing and started back down the logging trail a little too fast. One of the rocks in the road ripped the muffler apart when the wheels of the cruiser slid into a deep rut. The high-powered motor roared out in relief. He reached the paved highway and headed north toward Dry Run Hollow.


"Christ, wuzzat?" a man asked, quieting the talk in front of Constable Clippinger's home. The group, numbering at least forty, turned their attention to the west and Route 522. It was almost 8 P.M.

A cruiser, its siren blaring, rounded the curve near the men and stopped. Immediately behind it, three more state police cruisers rolled up, the shrill noise falling to a growl as sirens were switched off. Two young officers, milling freely before the arrival of the cars, grew a half-foot taller, sucking in their bellies and trotting to the second car in the caravan. The back door swung open.

"Friend, you're gonna see sumpin' now. That has gotta be Sherlock Holmes himself gettin' outta the back seat," one of the residents said to a companion. "Once saw ole Ike make a far less spectacular appearance than that in Paris. 'Course, he was only general of the armies then," he added, not

overwhelmed by the tall slim man who was now command-
ing a little too much attention from his subordinates.

"That's Lieutenant Mitarnowski," said a young officer
who had rejoined the civilians and overheard the remarks.

"Hot damn. How about that?" one lumberman in the
crowd spat out sarcastically. The officer, new to the area,
and unaware of the bitterness of the residents, was stunned
by the attitude. He quickly rejoined his fellow officers at the
cruiser.

"This is something else. They didn't teach us this at the
academy," the novice thought to himself, watching the civilians.

"Lieutenant," an officer called out to Mitarnowski,
"Ruegg said the best place to set up a command post is back
up the road. He said he would meet us there and we can get
this show under way." "Lead the way," Mitarnowski replied.

A sergeant had moved into the group of civilians, urging
them to follow him to the command post. Search parties
would be sent out systematically. In that way, the most
ground would be covered and they would have the best
possible chance of finding Mary and the kidnapper. "We're
going to get the bastard this time. He's pulled his last stunt,"
the sergeant swore.

Civilian cars followed the four police cruisers a half-mile
west of the constable's home, where Ruegg had already
stopped. It was a short distance from where the Broderick
children had gotten off the bus. Not only was the spot one of
the widest along the two-lane road; it provided excellent
radio reception.

Following a brief conversation between Ruegg and
Mitarnowski, the junior officer called for volunteers. He
was mobbed by the crowd of men anxious to do their part.
"What we need is a solid line of men along the road past the
Broderick home. We can't let the kidnapper sneak back out
of this pocket," Ruegg said, indicating the area east toward
Neelyton Mountain.

"OK, those who want to help, move up the dirt road. But for Christ sake, stay close. Don't lose sight of each other. Don't move into the woods. You don't have to make a lot of racket, but talk if you want to—we want him to know he's trapped. And don't get trigger-happy. Check out a noise before you fire. Remember Mary is in there with him," Ruegg warned.

Response from volunteers was far greater than anyone could have anticipated. The original number had nearly doubled with the arrival of more civilians. Many were teenagers, armed just as heavily as their elders. Some walked up the dirt road while others took off at a trot. Some were driven to the distant area by cars whose drivers returned for more. Other men piled into waiting cruisers.

While the civilians were being stationed, a call came through on the radio at the temporary command post: Check out Alternate Route 522 at a point identified as Dry Run Hollow. The name meant little to most of the officers who were spending their first night in the valley. But it sent the skin crawling on Ruegg. His thoughts turned back to July almost two years ago. Martha Yohn and her baby . . . the bottle shot from his mouth . . . bullets pumped into the car. . . .

Ruegg was moving toward a cruiser when he singled out Laskey, telling him to stick by Mitarnowski. "Assist where you can and keep him briefed. I'm headed for Dry Run Hollow," he added.

En route, Ruegg contacted Kline and Weigand by radio, and directed them to meet him at the remote spot. He wanted men familiar with the area if the kidnapper escaped to the east. Ruegg doubted seriously that the kidnapper had made his way back through the perimeter at the Broderick home.

Kline, who was south of Neelyton when the call came through, was the first of the trio to arrive. He was met by a half-dozen civilians who had discovered a brassiere.

Weigand, headed north from Decorum, pushed his foot to

the floor. "Damn," he said as the cruiser bounded over a knob south of the hollow. Ahead were the flashing lights of Kline's cruiser already parked along the road.

Moments after Weigand's cruiser came to a halt, Ruegg skidded in behind. "What have we got here?" Ruegg asked when he arrived at the knot of waiting men.

"I thought I heard a girl cry out up the trail, there," James McMullen, a member of the small search party, told the officer. "Then we found this," he continued, holding up the brassiere.

Ruegg took it and asked Kline to radio Lieutenant Mitarnowski. "Tell him what we've found, and ask him to send the dog as soon as it arrives," Ruegg directed.

"Let's stay down here for the moment. I don't want to ruin the scent for the dog when he gets here," he told the men gathered around him. "In the meantime spread out and see if we can find anything else in the immediate area."

Women's stockings, tissue paper, men's underwear used in hasty toiletry, and cloth rags were discovered as the men scoured the foothills leading up the mountainside.

Tom Stewart and his bloodhound arrived at the clearing just after the last daylight had disappeared from the valley.

"OK, everybody, come on back down here in the flat," Ruegg called. Excitement ran through the group. Now it would be easy to track the kidnapper and Mary—if the clothing was hers. But, Ruegg told Stewart, he wasn't sure. The trainer suggested that his dog try to pick up the scent on his own. "We could confuse him with the scent from the underwear," he said.

The investigator put the articles of clothing in a sample bag from a cruiser and sent them back to the command post.

The bloodhound immediately picked up a scent near the mountain logging trail. "The way he's acting, whoever went up that mountain did so not more than five or six hours ago," Stewart told the investigators. "We've got a hot scent and he's working."

"OK. This is what we'll do. Stewart, Plafcan, Kline,

Weigand and I will follow the dog up the trail," Ruegg told the group.

"The rest of you guys stay down here, but if you hear a shot, fan out in pairs and come running. Remember he's armed and he'll be trapped. We have men at the top of the mountain. Make a lot of racket," the inspector advised the civilians. "We want him to think there are at least a hundred of us. And don't use your flashlights when you stand still— you'll make a good target."

The small party of officers moved out behind dog and trainer. They had traveled less than 100 yards when the dog gave out its unique bark.

"Look here!" Stewart called out as he pulled the dog's leash and drew the animal to a stop. Fresh footprints were discovered at the mountain spring which cut across the logging trail—footprints of two persons headed eastward up the side of the mountain.

A closer inspection of the area revealed the prints were made by persons of like size. "Looks like whoever made these were traveling on," Ruegg said. "They didn't bother to jump the stream either . . . probably stepped into the water intentionally to kill the scent. Will that throw the dog off?" he asked Stewart.

"No. He'll pick up the scent again, and this time probably fresher and more distinctive. He could have been a little mixed up down there with all the tramping from those guys." Stewart pointed to the searchers.

"Good. Let's get going and see what we can find," Ruegg commanded.

The dog, straining at the leash again, didn't need a direction as he trotted off. Four of the five men had guns drawn as they moved up the steep mountainside. Stewart, armed with a sidegun, used both hands to hold the dog in check.

The logging trail melted into a cow path by the time the men and dog reached the half-way mark up the mountainside. The small trail wound around trees and rocks as it made its way upward. Still, the dog continued to strain on its leash.

But later, the trail turned sharply backward toward the valley, twisting and winding in the dense underbrush. The path was taking them down into Dry Run Hollow, about 100 feet north of the logging trail they had followed to ascend the mountain.

At a trot, the trainer and the officers followed the dog down the steep mountainside. The trail had taken a complete loop, and it was the only one the dog wanted to follow.

"May as well get started. The dog wants to go back up, and the longer we wait, the less chance we'll have," Stewart told the investigators.

More than forty men at the foot of the mountain watched the lights flicker as the five again made the trek to the summit. An hour later the five men and dog returned, having taken the same route again.

"You might radio Mitarnowski, no more hikes up the mountain tonight," Stewart announced. "The dog's feet are too sore. One of his paws has been cut on something and it's bleeding, probably from straining at the leash all night," he concluded.

With the information passed on, Ruegg announced to Stewart and his fellow officers that the hunt would be called off for the night. Volunteers were left near the trail just in case the kidnapper decided to come that way again.

# THE SECOND DAY   *Thursday, May 12, 1966*

In Camp Hill, a suburb of Harrisburg, FBI Agent Terry Anderson and his wife, Margie, were sleeping soundly. Anderson, forty-one, was a native of Nebraska, but assigned to duty in Pennsylvania. He had been with the Bureau for fifteen years and, like all agents, easily adapted to his new territory; he soon came to love the Keystone State. He had said that he wanted to live here for the rest of his life.

On Thursday morning—barely after midnight—he was awakened by the phone ringing. He turned on the lamp and picked up the receiver. He listened for a minute, then said, "I'll be there in an hour."

Margie, also awakened by the ringing, looked at him expectantly. "Who was that?"

Anderson swung out of bed. "The state police, calling from Shade Gap. They're bringing us in on the Broderick case. They think the kidnapper escaped on the Turnpike, couple of miles from where the girl was abducted." He paused and waited for the trail of questions he knew would follow.

"But that's not your district. Where's Tom Dolan? That's his area, isn't it?" she asked in what she knew was a futile attempt to keep Terry home.

"Not available. He's in Philadelphia at a firearms school." he replied as he started to dress. "Anyhow, it's only about fifty miles west of here and I'll be back before long," he promised.

Margie headed for the kitchen. Coffee would keep him awake during the drive to Shade Gap. It wasn't necessary for Terry to pack. The routine had been repeated many times before and a complete change of clothes for at least five days was stored in the trunk of his car, along with a large supply of ammunition and a variety of weapons and tools.

It was nearly 3:00 A.M. when Terry arrived in the small village of Burnt Cabins, a short distance from Shade Gap. Police cruisers and private cars lined the roadside with the headlights burning. When he turned left at Burnt Cabins, an unmarked state police cruiser fell in behind and kept pace until Terry turned off the road at Decorum. A winding road brought him to the command post.

He found a spot to park the car and stepped from the vehicle into crowds of civilians and police. "Someone is going to get killed," he thought, noting the determination on every face he saw. Everyone was armed.

Then he spotted Trooper Rockwell. This was Tom Dolan's territory and Terry was only slightly acquainted with Rocky. Rocky saw Terry slowly edging his way through the crowd. There were no words of greeting when Rocky spoke, "Somethin', isn't it?" Terry shook his head in disbelief at the size of the armed posse. "Never saw anything like this in my entire life," he replied. "Where's Dolan?" asked Rocky.

"He's at school in Philly," Terry replied. "He'll probably get here later."

"Anyhow, glad you're here to help. Want me to introduce you to the lieutenant?" Rocky asked.

"Not yet. Think I'll look around a bit and get a cup of coffee, thanks." Terry moved off.

He was glad to overhear a conversation about a portable

land base radio station being set up at the Shade Gap picnic grounds. At least it would provide a better place to park and set up operations in a dry area. It was misting rain as he reported to Lieutenant Mitarnowski at 3:30 A.M.

In Chambersburg, the county seat of Franklin County southeast of Shade Gap, Trooper Milton Brown was issuing instructions at the barracks. Barely 5 A.M., the sun had not yet risen.

"Herb, you and Swider go in one car and Alexiou and Frazer will go in another. Report to the command post at the picnic grounds. We'll send word you are on the way. "I don't have to tell you again, this guy is dangerous. If it's the same guy that's been doing the shooting, he can pick out a gnat's eye at 100 yards. Just remember, there ain't no live heroes," Brown cautioned as the sleepy quartet trooped out of the barracks.

The cruiser moved slowly through the deserted streets of the county seat. A borough officer gave a salute as they passed the downtown section. The sleeping little communities of St. Thomas and Fort Loudon swept by the windows of the car. It began to rain. The radio in the cruiser continued to provide constant reports on the officers arriving from other stations throughout the south central part of the state. There was little conversation.

At the command post, the four officers put on their rain gear and walked the last several hundred feet to the large metal building now housing the growing operation.

After reporting to Sergeant William Kimmel, they joined 100 other state police officers at breakfast.

Troopers Herb and Swider had arrived at Shade Gap at 6:00 A.M. Sitting under a pavilion with officers from Huntingdon and McConnellsburg, they took in most of the conversation from the men who had spent the last twelve hours in the area. The men were tired, sleepy and wet. They welcomed the replacements streaming in from Altoona, Chambersburg, York, Harrisburg, Carlisle, Huntingdon and as far west as Bedford.

Most conversation centered upon the uncanny disappearance of the kidnapper and his victim, and the failure of the bloodhound to pick up the trail.

Theories ran the gamut from a total fake to the realization that the girl might already be dead and buried in the rugged mountains. Still, no one was ready to give up the search, not even those scheduled for relief. They would be back.

The most popular idea was that the kidnapper had escaped by car, using the nearby Turnpike as an escape route. But they realized that until this could be proved, the search would go on in the immediate area.

"You two patrol 641 from Orbisonia to Neelyton. Check anything and everything," Sergeant Kimmel told Herb and Swider. "And keep in touch with the command post for further orders. Call in every time you make a new swing over the area," he added.

"You like the new description they gave us on the kidnapper?" Swider asked Herb, as they buckled in and moved from the picnic grounds.

"Can you imagine? He ain't too tall and he ain't too short. He ain't too fat and he ain't too skinny. He was wearing certain clothes when he made the snatch, but surely wouldn't be wearing them now. He's got a gruff voice, but it's as normal as yours and mine."

"Hell, the only difference between him and us is that he's got Mary Lou and we don't. And the clincher—that he's armed with a rifle, a shotgun or a handgun, or maybe all of them—hell, that fits everybody I've seen since we came here," Herb lamented.

Swider turned left at the main highway and drove in the direction of Shade Gap and Orbisonia. The rain had slowed to a drizzle.

Dozens of vehicles, filled with volunteers on the way to

the campgrounds, passed the slow-moving police cruiser. The occupants, young and old alike, were armed with guns, their barrels plainly visible.

The officers were on the second swing between Orbisonia and Neelyton when the radio announced that a suspicious man was seen near Neelyton at the base of the mountain. He was said to be on foot in the woods opposite the command post. The two were ordered to the site to investigate.

But a two-hour search, covering more than twenty miles of unpaved roads, turned up nothing. Residents of the area reported seeing no one in the vicinity. All assured the troopers that they had been on the lookout constantly since the kidnapping occurred.

A radio call to the command post put the pair on another hunt. They were ordered to return to the picnic grounds and pick up a resident of the area, who would accompany them to places where the kidnapper and his victim could hide.

The "resident" turned out to be Charlie. "Just call me Charlie. I was with another policeman yesterday and we sort of fizzled out. All we did was rip the muffler out of the police car and make a lot of racket," the guide said as he stuck out his hand to greet them. Herb and Swider shook his hand with misgivings, noting his reckless handling of a double-barrel shotgun.

Charlie saw the look and said, "Don't you worry none. Bessie here ain't loaded. I took the shells out before you came."

"OK. That's our car beside the pavilion. Jump in and as soon as we get coffee, we'll be on our way," Herb said.

In ten minutes, the trio pulled away from the command post.

"About a mile up the road here there's some vacant cottages," Charlie told them, pointing the barrel of the shotgun toward Orbisonia. "Anybody who had a mind to could hide out there forever from you strangers," he said proudly. "Strangers" sounded not unlike "foreigners" to the two officers; they were stationed less than forty miles away.

The cruiser jolted and rocked in the ruts when Swider turned off the paved highway into a narrow drive. The vehicle slid in mud when he braked in front of a cottage a short distance from the highway. The doors and the windows of the weathered frame building were boarded up, giving an appearance of a small fortress.

It didn't require a genius to realize how easy it would be to pick off anyone approaching from the road. Swider and Herb slid down on the front seat to provide a smaller target.

"Too late to back up now. You take the left and I'll take the right. Stay here and guard our flank, Charlie," Herb directed.

"Sure. OK. You go ahead," Charlie replied.

Both troopers left the cruiser and separated with drawn guns. They approached the building from the sides, away from the threatening front windows and door. A thorough search of the dwelling revealed all boards across the openings in place, lessening the threat of ambush from inside. Peering between slits of the boards, the officers made sure the cottage was empty.

When they returned to the car, Herb told Charlie that it would be nice to know earlier if the next cottage was so close to the road. "Rather not park out in the open like that again. If someone had been inside, it could've been bad."

"Sorry about that," Charlie apologized. "Didn't figure you would drive up on the place that fast. See if I can't do better the next time." He directed the troopers down the same road where another cottage was located.

But it too was deserted, as were three other cabins, with no sign that they had been used for months.

"Where else do you want to take us?" Swider asked when they returned to the cruiser.

"Well, there's this old farm back aways from the Mountain Foot Road. Far as I know, it's been empty for a couple of years. And it's near where the Blake lady was attacked," Charlie offered.

"Tell us about her. What happened?" Herb asked to pass the time driving to the farm.

"Turn here," Charlie directed as he completed a detailed description of the attack which occurred nearly two years before. His narrative brought the officers back to reality. The quarry they sought was dangerous!

"How far back from this road is the farm?" Swider asked, driving the car slowly through rows of trees and bush.

"A short ways. As far as I can recall, this is the only road into it. The farm goes straight back into the woods, there." Charlie said.

The rain suddenly increased to a downpour as the vehicle entered a clearing. Swider stopped the car as a farmhouse and two barns came into view.

"You see what I see?" Swider asked suspiciously.

"Yeah. Tire tracks going in and none coming out," Herb confirmed.

Swider slid the cruiser into reverse and swung the wheel, stopping the car at a ninety-degree angle with the road. "This is the only road in?" he asked Charlie again.

"Yes. Anyone in there has got to come out this way," he replied while he calmly but deliberately pulled his shotgun off the floor of the car.

"You stay here, Charlie, and make sure no one comes past. Swider, you take the rifle and I'll take the shotgun and we'll see who the hell is up there," Herb said. Swider and Charlie agreed.

The troopers grabbed their raincoats and guns from the trunk of the cruiser and moved toward the nearest building. They stopped short, about 100 feet ahead of the parked cruiser.

"Let's separate," Herb suggested. They approached the barn from opposite ends. Swider stood outside the barn door for a few seconds, counting silently the time he figured it would take Herb to reach the other end.

Then he burst in through the barn door with the rifle leveled chest high. A moment later Herb entered from the far end. It was dark inside the building. Both men quickly stepped out of the doorways and leaned against the walls until they could see.

They checked out the barn. Nothing there—but piles of hay and bales of straw. The only sound came from a pigeon high in the rafters.

The two men left the barn to tackle the house. A relic, it stood forlorn and abandoned. What had once been a farmhouse was now a wreck; broken windows, rotten stairs, sagging porch. The troopers hesitated for a moment; each realized that the house could be harboring an armed kidnapper.

Once inside, they found the interior of the building was as badly decayed as the exterior. Ceilings were broken, plaster chunks were scattered about, bare cords dangled in place of lights. They searched the first floor then cautiously made their way to the second.

Searching one room, Herb checked the closets. Opening a door, he heard a sound and wheeled around, pointing his gun. Ready to pull the trigger, he looked up and saw Swider, also ready to shoot. The men trembled, thinking how very close they had come to blasting each other.

Silence in the house. Then, a sound from the attic. Both men strained to hear it again, but it was not repeated.

Convinced that they had found the Mountain Man, Swider and Herb ran for the attic stairs. What they found, instead, was a ladder leading to an opening in the ceiling. Herb was the first one up, motioning to Swider to stand guard at the bottom.

The attic was like the rest of the house—barren, deserted, covered with cobwebs and dust. The noise came from either the flock of pigeons nesting in the corner—or from tree limbs brushing against the roof. Herb left the attic.

They had one more building to search—the second barn. Again, nothing. They left the grounds and walked back to the cruiser.

"Good you came out of the house when you did. I was just about to come up and see what the hell was keeping you," Charlie greeted them through a partially opened window of the cruiser.

"Just as well you didn't. We didn't need another gun back there," Herb said. "Besides, it's empty."

Then the officers studied the tire tracks. A single footprint was discovered along the left side of the tracks, giving the officers a good idea of what happened before they arrived. Apparently another car had driven to the building and the driver opened the door, stepped out, and changed his mind. The car probably backed out of the driveway in the same tracks and left the scene. It was impossible to link the tracks to a specific type of vehicle.

Swider radioed the command post and received orders to patrol along Route 522 between Burnt Cabins and Shade Gap.

It was mid-morning of the second day. Troopers Gus Alexiou and Bob Derwin, accompanied by Guy Price, patrolled the tight corner of the valley near Mary Lou's home.

The troopers had been trained in the logic of police detection work, but this case offered little of it. The only common conclusion the trio reached was that the Mountain Man was a native of the area.

The patrol car made its way through the rain around the small perimeter of the Broderick home, encountering dozens of armed civilians. All were accounted for by the guide, Guy Price, who sat in the back seat of the cruiser.

Price recognized the high school boys, let out of school to join in the search, and youths from Huntingdon College, who too were given permission to help in the hunt.

He listed name after name of the people who had taken up arms in the pursuit of the kidnapper and his victim. He told the officers he couldn't think of a single family from the area not represented in the hunt.

The great majority of those he recognized were excellent shots. "I'd match these men up against any rifle team in the nation," Price commented. "When we find him, he's a dead man," he added with conviction.

"I'm glad you guys are on our side," Alexiou commented. A chill went up his spine at the thought of what was to come when the identity of the kidnapper was discovered. Price's hate was obvious.

"Look. This is getting us nowhere. You know everybody in the search. Is there anywhere else we could go where the kidnapper could hide, or dispose of Mary Lou's body if she is dead?" Alexiou asked Price.

"Well, there's lots of abandoned places along the foot of Neelyton Mountain. If someone was gonna dispose of a body, I know of some wells that would make likely places. Maybe the S.O.B. who took Mary Lou knows them too."

"OK. Wait till I check with the command post and see if it's okay to bust out of here," Alexiou said, reaching for the radio. He was told to take off and drove east, toward Decorum.

"Turn left here," Price directed. "We'll have to park the car and walk back to the mountain," he continued.

"Pick as much grass and weeds to step on as you can or you'll be so bogged down in the mud you'll never get out," he advised the officers as he stepped from the back seat into the steadily falling rain. "It's about a half-mile walk across the fields—straight back that way near the foot of the mountain," Price said as he pointed to the gray expanse in the distance.

"Lead the way. We're with you." Alexiou told the guide.

The two officers caught up with Price at the end of the field, where the first trees of the mountain offered firm ground.

"Why in the hell would anyone build a well back here, where the only way you could reach it is by helicopter or a swamp buggy?" Derwin asked.

"Used to be a family here, but the place burned down," Price answered.

"Probably the best thing that ever happened to them," Derwin said.

The trio moved into the woods, in search of the ruins of the house. It was less than 300 feet from where they entered. Soaked boards, weathered with the years, were thrown recklessly over the opening of the well, estimated to be more than 15 feet deep to the water level. Flashlights directed into the pit revealed metal sheets lying near the bottom.

After informing the command post of what they had discovered, Alexiou was advised that more officers would be dispatched, as well as ropes. Price agreed to retrace his steps and lead the contingent to the well, while Alexiou and Derwin stood guard.

Price returned shortly, accompanied by six officers and two more civilians. The local people felt that the well was at least ten to fifteen feet deeper than the metal sheets.

Price and one of his neighbors dropped into the well, after ropes had been fastened around their waists. The others anxiously followed their progress.

The metal sheets were lifted out of the hole, revealing only muddy water and part of a tree limb. Grappling hooks were used to probe the well, after the limb was removed. They found nothing.

Disheartened, the men gathered up their supplies, covered the opening with planks and the metal sheets, and trudged back across the muddy fields to their cars.

"Maybe she isn't dead after all," Alexiou commented on the way back to the command post.


"Wish to hell someone would print a program," Bob Cox told his fellow newsman Ken Peiffer. "Can't tell the cops from the civilians anymore since they shed their uniforms and changed to hunting clothing." The pair made their way up to the Shade Gap Picnic Grounds. It was noon.

"Know what you mean. Saw some of the gang from the Chambersburg barracks, but hardly recognized them in civvies," Peiffer said.

"Let's see if they know anything we don't; but let's eat first," Cox directed.

After eating, Bob Cox called the news desk of the Chambersburg *Public Opinion* from a nearby phone booth.

"Come back to the office about 5 P.M. and bring Ken along. Seems like the wire services want us to feed them," Cox was told.

After locating Peiffer at the command post, where more than 300 men had gathered for a briefing from Mitarnowski, the pair decided they would split and cover more territory.

"Think I'll go back and talk to all the other victims this afternoon, while you go along on the cross-country hike," Cox suggested.

"Suits me. Say 'Hi' to Ned and the rest of them for me when you see them," Peiffer said as he unbuckled his camera to get a shot of Mitarnowski. The lieutenant was walking from the command post with an assistant, looking for an advantageous spot to address the crowd.

Cox walked toward the field where he had left his VW bus parked long before dawn, got in and drove toward the Price home.

Peiffer joined the hundreds who were lined up behind the Broderick home for a cross-country sweep, designed to cover every inch of ground, starting from where the girl was kidnapped to Alternate Route 522.

Two hundred civilians, accompanied by sixty-five policemen, were told to line up shoulder to shoulder along the dirt road, and at a signal, move east across the countryside. A stern warning was given not to advance ahead of the man at each side, and keep all guns unloaded. "The kidnapper is not going to be found in this sweep. What we want to find are clues—anything Mary might have dropped or the kidnapper might have discarded," Mitarnowski said. He could have saved his breath.


Herb put the massive sweep in perspective after it was over. "It was damn scary. Every man in the party was primed and ready to blow apart anything that moved. A guy next to me said, 'If I see the son-of-a-bitch, I'll blow his head off.' And yet, no one knew what the kidnapper looked like, his build, his size, his appearance, what he wore, nothing. Next to him another man slid a shell into a deer rifle. Down the line the same thing was repeated. Christ, it was like a footrace to see who covered the most ground in the fastest time. By the time we were one-quarter of the way down the first hill, the line curved outward 50 to 75 yards and was getting worse by the minute. We lost control.

"When rifles and shotguns were waved around with the safeties off, a lot of staties abandoned the search, for fear of not only their lives, but for nearly everyone there."

Alexiou, generally controlled under most circumstances, said of the cross-country search, "I got the hell out of there when those damn clowns started running ahead and waving their loaded guns. Those guys were out for blood—anybody's blood. Someone was going to get his head blown off. I didn't want it to be me. I didn't even want to be a witness. Weird, it was. In all that mountain climbing and cross-country racing, there wasn't one cut or sprain. Just blisters. Lord, the blisters," he said.

In the middle of the afternoon, cars, trucks, motorcycles and even a helicopter converged on the area of Neelyton Mountain east of Decorum. A man in a white shirt had been seen sprinting through the woods near the bottomland. The traffic jam was impossible. Out of every car window, a head peered toward the mountainside, which was shrouded in mist.

The occupants were yelling for blood, so caught up in the mass-kill hysteria that it sounded like a chant. The mob was nearing madness; reason was abandoned.

Only through the quick action of the police, spreading the word received from the helicopter pilot that their intended victim was a policeman, was certain disaster avoided. They stopped vehicles and blocked side roads to prevent the mob from chasing across the fields. The realization that their intended victim was not the kidnapper disgusted the hunters—and enraged them. They wanted blood.

The officer spotted in the woods was following a lead given by the command post. He had been sighted by a passerby, but his companion in full uniform had not been, leading to the rumor that "some nut is running through the woods in a white shirt."

Swider and Herb, ordered to return to the command post, picked up Lieutenant Tittler. He directed a search of abandoned wells off Alternate Route 522, again at the foot of Neelyton Mountain. Cox, who had just finished visiting with Jessie Price, got the high sign from Herb as he drove past and the newsman fell in line.

One more police car moving along the road already choked with police and civilian vehicles did not attract attention. By the time the cruiser parked along the two-lane road and the newsman stopped behind it, word was received over the CB radios now in use that the "suspect in the white shirt" was another in a long line of false leads. And traffic had thinned to a point where no one showed interest in the four men who were carrying ropes and grappling hooks walking across the fields toward the foot of the mountain.

The well was dragged first with no results. Then Herb and Swider climbed down into the excavation to the water level. Again, with grappling hooks, debris was removed from the well, but the searchers once more came up with nothing.

The four, soaked with rain, covered with mud to their waists, scratched from barbed wire and generally miserable, were met by two carloads of newsmen who came upon the parked cars and decided to await the return of the occupants. The physical discomfort of the four, coupled with the discouragement of still another fruitless search, caused the newsmen to be met with hostility.

The displeasure of newsmen rebuffed in search of a story led to an exchange of words; they said they would retaliate by following every police car thereafter. They felt the officers were less than candid, that they were attempting to suppress news.

The tenor of questions and remarks of the newspapermen only resulted in the police clamming up about Cox's identity, further widening the gap already existing between the press and police.

Swider accompanied Cox back to the command post in his VW bus, while Herb and Tittler returned in the patrol car. The two carloads of newsmen faithfully followed, tailgating the police cruiser.

Upon arriving, Swider was met by an FBI agent and the two left in the agent's car to search a site reported to be quicksand, this time at the base of Shade Mountain. It too proved to be a fruitless hunch.

Herb fared better. After returning with Tittler, he was assigned to desk duty, where he gained a knowledge of the scope of the operation.

"I went through so many reports, and assigned so many officers to follow so many leads, I really didn't think it was possible. Every one proved false."

At 11 P.M., more than 100 copies of a photograph of Mary Lou Broderick were made available for police, investigators and newsmen at the command post. Also made available— for police only—were photographs of three prime suspects, one of whom was a Chambersburg resident, the top suspect at the time.

City and state police located and interrogated the man. He was released after hours of questioning, but placed under surveillance.

The other two suspects had perfect alibis and before dawn Friday, police were back where they started—with nothing.

Long after nightfall, more than 100 policemen and FBI agents continued their door-to-door questioning of every household in the area. Many were marked for visits again the next day and the next, until every man in the valley was accounted for. But these inquiries turned up absolutely nothing. Suspicions, guesses and theories of the valley inhabitants were compiled and cross-checked against those of previous investigations—all to no avail. The Chambersburg state police substation, with its powerful radio tower atop Tuscarora Mountain, relayed messages from car to car when their radios were unable to do so.

Volunteer firemen, off-duty policemen and many others, from the far reaches of the state and from adjacent states, offered their services and were directed to report to the Shade Gap command post for assignment. Most were genuine offers of food and drink for the searchers, women who were willing to babysit while those familiar with the area were busy in the search or helping in other ways. All calls were received courteously even though the officer answering the call at times was amused.

Corporal Ray Hussack, Chambersburg, recalled two such calls. "A man from the Waynesboro area asked permission to join the hunt and to go into the area with his 'dowser branch' which he claimed was successful in locating water. He said he could also find anything buried in the area. We feared that Mary Lou was dead by now so we sent him over.

"Another call came from a woman who said she had a vision. She said that if we laid a clock on the map of the area and followed the hands of the clock, we would find Mary's grave. I quickly referred her to the command post, not even bothering to ask which hand of the clock to follow, how far, where to point twelve o'clock or anything else."

# THE THIRD DAY   *Friday, May 13, 1966*

The sun was just coming up as Peiffer drove up Timmons Mountain. The sleep he had just had did little to refresh him from the constant vigil since Mary Lou's kidnapping. "I must have shot and developed a hundred pictures over the last thirty-six hours, and printed half that many," he thought to himself. The roar of the underpowered car grew as he down-shifted on the steep road.

Nearing the summit, he glanced in the rearview mirror and saw two state police cruisers approaching rapidly. He rounded the curve at the top of the mountain and pulled to the right to allow them to pass. Both were off like a shot when they passed his slow-moving car. He did not recognize any of them—they were all out of uniform.

Twenty minutes later, after chugging over Neelyton Mountain into the valley, Peiffer stopped near the command post. He guessed fifty cars were parked at the picnic grounds, half of which were police cruisers.

As he unloaded two cameras and stuffed his pockets with film, he noticed familiar faces in the group; Ned Price was there, limping on his artificial leg as he carried a steaming cup of coffee to a picnic table. He recognized Isaac Frehn, the school bus driver who dropped Mary Lou and her brothers and sisters off almost into the arms of the kidnapper.

Frehn was with Arthur Devlin, Price's nephew, already seated and drinking coffee. Next to him sat Charles Yohn, whose wife and baby had come under the Mountain Man's fire nearly two years ago.

And then he saw Broderick, father of the young victim. As a newsman, Peiffer was accustomed to seeing tragedy but he had never seen such hopelessness on the face of a man.

Several minutes later, he walked to the nearby command post and talked his way into an experience unique in his years as a reporter and photographer.

"Need someone familiar with the area to go along with some officers and Mr. Broderick on a search party," an officer called out from the gaping doors of the command post. Peiffer volunteered before any of the other men could respond.

"You're elected. Come with me," the officer said before noticing that Peiffer was carrying a camera. "Just who and what the hell are you?" the officer asked when he saw the equipment.

"I'm a reporter from Chambersburg, but I've spent the last two years in Shade Gap," Peiffer stretched the truth to fit the occasion.

"OK," the officer said. "Join Broderick and these two officers, but don't get cute with those cameras," he said with obvious misgivings.

Peiffer needed no urging as he opened the rear door of the cruiser for Broderick.

As the vehicle moved out of the parking area, Broderick was the first to speak. "I believe Mary's alive. I just have the feeling that nothing's happened to her. I don't know why. I just feel that way. She's alive," he rambled, receiving false assurances from the other three, who were now of the opposite opinion. Too much time had passed since the kidnapping, with no word or sight of her.

Police were working on the theory that the girl was dead and were searching for her body, as well as clothing or other clues. They held little hope that they were wrong.

"She knows the roads around here, but she'd be lost in the mountains," Broderick stated as a matter of fact. "If she's still around and can find her way back to a road, she'll make it home, you can bet on it," he continued when silence was the only response.

"Sure she will," the driver finally said. "And if she's still up there in the mountains, you can bet we'll find her before long," he added with false hope in his voice.

When the cruiser turned into a dirt road, the conversation changed to the immediate situation. "Damn," the driver said as the car slid into ruts partially filled with water. Now that all four wheels were locked into deep ruts, it was impossible to move the vehicle onto the firm ground between the lanes of travel. Mud splattered the windshield.

Progress was slow as the cruiser bounced along the road toward the mountain east of Shade Gap. "Don't have too far to go now," Broderick said when the vehicle had traveled about a half-mile from the paved highway. With the exception of the driver, all eyes searched the surrounding landscape for any signs of movement.

"You sure this place is deserted?" the driver asked Broderick. The cruiser rounded a sharp bend in the road and braked a short distance from their destination—an old frame home and a large barn.

"Yes. No one comes back here except kids hunting a place to make out," Broderick answered.

"Right. Let's take the barn first," the trooper said as he stopped the cruiser. One hundred feet away were the gaping doors of the dilapidated structure. With slight hesitation, the four headed for the ramp in front of the barn.

In the dim light of the interior, a dozen pigeons took flight, alarming the men who could barely see. Instinct directed four hands to their weapons.

Calm returned in seconds and the search of the barn was begun in earnest, with Peiffer accompanying a trooper into the lower level of the barn, and Broderick going with the other officer into the loft. A thorough search revealed nothing.

From the shadows of the open barn doors the four appraised the house, its windows darkened by drawn blinds.

"You and Broderick stay by the cruiser while we check this out," one officer advised, moving away from his companion in the general direction of the building.

Peiffer unstrapped his camera and took a light meter reading. He took a few shots of the men approaching the house before he and Broderick moved to the car.

The officers circled the building in opposite directions. They tried windows and doors in vain, but couldn't open any. Finally, one managed to pry open a window and was boosted inside by his companion. The other officer entered the house when his companion opened the door from the inside.

The wait was getting to Broderick. He puffed nervously on a cigarette and said to Peiffer, "I just have a feeling they're not in the area, unless the dirty devil has her locked up some place." Then he fell silent and walked toward a thicket at the rear of the car.

Peiffer considered Broderick's behavior. Here was a situation that didn't follow any pattern. There had been no demands; Broderick was unemployed. He had no money to buy his daughter's safety, even if there had been a ransom note.

Broderick returned from his trip into the thickets and was told that the house was clean, with nothing amiss. "Looks like it's been unoccupied for months," one officer said.

The driver pointed the car further into the woods toward a densely wooded area that could provide shelter from the elements, as well as concealment from searchers. En route to the area, the officers decided they would split up, with one going with Broderick, and the other with Peiffer.

"If either of us sees anything, fire a shot into the air and the other will come running. If help is needed, fire two quick shots," the driver said to his companion, who agreed with a nod.

All four men had guns drawn as they searched for anything that might provide a clue to Mary's whereabouts. For more than an hour Peiffer and his companion, always within sight of each other, searched the area.

"It's amazing we can't even find a gum wrapper or a cigarette butt," the policeman commented as he suggested they move back to the cruiser.

Before they returned to the command post, they dropped Broderick off at his home, where he was greeted by his young children. The Brodericks were huddled on the front porch as the cruiser moved away.

Peiffer joined the long line of men at the Shade Gap pavilion where lunch was being served. He picked up two ham and cheese sandwiches and a Pepsi, and walked to a picnic table under the shelter of a large pine, searching for Cox. He wanted to relate the events of the morning and to hand over his exposed film. To his amazement, he didn't recognize a single face among the several hundred people milling around the area. They were all strangers.

Peiffer returned the empty bottle to the wooden carrying cases stacked neatly at one picnic table, and walked to his parked car to replenish his supply of film. He watched the cars arrive in the early afternoon, filled with volunteers who were skipping work as well as school to assist. He caught glimpses of license plates from Maryland, West Virginia and Ohio, and realized that either dedication or curiosity lay behind the reasons these people would travel such distances.

"If a person were to collect all the guns and ammunition being carried in the area right now, he could start a small war of his own," Peiffer observed, opening a conversation with one of the officers.

Between swallows of soft drink and sandwich, the trooper replied, "Small, hell. You could start the real thing on a grand scale." He wearily shook his head in response to Peiffer's question if anything else had turned up. "Not a damn thing. It's like the wheels of the car this morning—spinning but going no place. The son-of-a-bitch just up and disappeared as if he never existed. Man, I've been on some good cases before, but this takes the cake."

Peiffer and the trooper were leaning on the fender of the cruiser when a call came over the police radio. "Anyone familiar with Franklin County, especially the area around Spring Run, report to the unmarked patrol car along Route 641, midway between Shade Gap and Neelyton."

Peiffer looked, the officer nodded, and both got into the cruiser. The trooper radioed he had the man they were looking for and headed the cruiser toward the rendezvous point. Within five minutes, they stopped behind a blue Ford sedan parked along the road.

When the trooper and Peiffer walked to the side of the Ford, a man dressed in a trench coat asked Peiffer for identification, and was satisfied with the Chambersburg, Franklin County address on his ID cards.

"You'll do. Here's the deal. We received a tip about two brothers living in a cabin in the Spring Run area at a place called Mountain Green. We're going over there to check it out," the trench-coated man said. Peiffer's urge to smile was stifled when the man identified himself as an FBI agent. He reminded Peiffer of a movie spy, but by the tone of his voice, was obviously in charge.

His demeanor commanded respect, especially when he told the officer to follow his car and directed Peiffer to enter the rear of the Ford. "Turn around and go back toward the command post," he directed the driver. "We've picked up some unwanted company."

A number of cars loaded with newsmen had stopped behind the two police vehicles. Most of the cars had the familiar whip antennas; they were able to monitor both police and CB calls.

When the driver swung the Ford around in the road, the civilians followed suit, turning around and falling in line, giving the appearance of a funeral procession traveling slowly west on Route 641. The entourage turned into the picnic grounds; only the two lead police cars moved close to the command post, where civilian cars were forbidden to park.

The trooper parked the marked cruiser and joined Peiffer and the other two agents in the unmarked vehicle. After a fifteen-minute wait, they rolled slowly out of the picnic grounds and headed toward Spring Run, some ten miles away.

When the vehicle neared the original rendezvous point, the driver suddenly braked and pulled onto the shoulder. "Gotta let the convoy pass," he said to the other three men. A line of Army jeeps passed, moving toward the command post. In addition, several personnel carriers and canopied trucks filled with soldiers were included in the convoy. "It's the National Guard unit from Huntingdon. They were called in to assist in the search," the driver said.

The cruiser moved ahead after the convoy passed, and the ride over the mountain into Franklin County passed quickly.

When the vehicle entered the small settlement of Spring Run, the driver turned right onto a secondary road which paralleled the eastern base of the mountain. Less than a half-mile south of Route 641, they made another right turn onto a dirt road leading into an apple orchard. Still moving at nearly fifty miles per hour, the cruiser splashed muddy water high into the air. At the southwestern point of the orchard, they came to a barn where two men were working. The car jolted to a stop and the FBI agent stepped out to talk to the pair.

Just then, Peiffer heard a helicopter hovering overhead. The two men speaking with the agent kept glancing at the chopper. One made a general indication with his hand toward the mountain.

When the agent returned to the car, he spoke into the

mike and told the operator of the helicopter to locate the home of the suspect, and to keep on the lookout for anyone who might be on foot. The cruiser roared ahead, turning left toward Neelyton.

Only the mountain separated the cruiser now from a point directly east of Dry Run Hollow, the place where the dogs were led in circles by the kidnapper the night of the abduction—the same spot where the sniper had barricaded the road with logs and pumped bullets into the car driven by Mrs. Yohn. Peiffer's pulse accelerated.

Within minutes, the vehicle stopped at a wooden gate in front of an old house. The men scanned the area for several minutes; then the driver was instructed to return to the barn where the two men were working. The agent wanted to make certain the property they were looking at was the home of the suspect.

In minutes they were at the barn. The agent in charge got out of the car, talked to the two men again and returned to the cruiser. "There are two houses back there. A smaller one in addition to the one we saw must be located further back into the woods," the agent said to Peiffer and the driver. "Let's go back," he ordered.

As the cruiser neared the house for the second time, the 'copter pilot radioed, "Just spotted some guy pop out of the door of the house, look up at us and then take off into the mountain on foot." The agent grabbed the microphone, ordered the pilot to keep the man in sight, then radioed a call to a backup unit which had followed but stayed in the area of Spring Run. The cruiser was directed to stay in the area of the orchard and seal off any possible escape.

The unmarked car reached the wooden gate, swerved off the road alongside the fence and circled the house. When the car was opposite the first house, the second and smaller structure came into view. "Stop over there beside that log pile," the agent directed, indicating a location several hundred feet away from the dwellings.

The three law enforcement men approached the dwelling

from opposite directions. Peiffer, alone in the car, was dropping shells into his .32 caliber pistol when he saw movements in the woods beyond the agent and one trooper. He was about to call out when they stopped and the agent moved toward a man coming out of the woods, carrying an ax over his shoulder.

Although Peiffer was unable to hear, he watched the conversation being carried on between the agent and the woodsman. Then the agent motioned for Peiffer to come forward. When he was within earshot, the agent called out to Peiffer, "Find the other man and get him here on the double. Then go back to the cruiser and answer the radio if there's a call."

Peiffer took off on a run and caught the other agent just as he was rounding the building on the opposite side from the officers and the woodsman.

Within a few minutes, the young trooper returned to the cruiser. "This guy looks like a good prospect," he said. "You won't believe the guns in there. Got a good feeling about this. They found several pairs of women's pants and an old Halloween mask. This is the guy, all right. Christ, they found an arsenal of guns, and rubber topcoats and boots— the whole damn works," he went on.

The first agent came out of the house carefully carrying a rifle wrapped in a cloth. "It's the same type of gun used in the other shootings over the past two years," he explained.

A third cruiser skidded to a halt beside the group, and Detective Broscius stepped out. A few minutes later, the agents and the detective appeared with the suspect and walked directly to Peiffer, waiting by the unmarked car.

The suspect was a man who hid his age. Peiffer guessed him to be between fifty and sixty, muscular, with intense blue eyes. He wore a baseball cap, plaid shirt and tan trousers. He was placed in the center of the back seat and strapped in by a seat belt. "Don't want you to fall out," Detective Broscius said.

Those were the only words spoken, except to tell the

driver to head for the command post. The first agent sat on one side and the detective on the other as the cruiser moved away.

When the vehicle left Franklin County and came into Neelyton, the agent told the driver to pull off behind another parked cruiser. "This is where you leave, Peiffer. Thanks for your help, but it would be better if we didn't have a civilian along when we get back."

Peiffer switched cars and arrived at the command post just minutes behind the car with the suspect. He was in time to see the cruiser pull out with the suspect again between two men. Later, he asked Lieutenant Mitarnowski how they made out with the interrogation.

"What interrogation? I don't know what you're talking about. We haven't got any suspects."

Meanwhile Cox turned his VW bus into the command post, swerved the wheel to miss one hole in the dirt road and managed to drop into a deeper one. He uttered a choice oath when his pants left the seat of the bus and slammed down with a sickening thud. He got out of the bus, reached the command post and started hunting for Peiffer.

A half-hour hunt was fruitless, and when he discovered another search would not be going out until after lunch, Cox decided to visit Ned Price. He would return by 1:00 P.M. to catch Peiffer or at least be in time to join the search.

When he pulled up in front of the Price residence, Cox noticed slats of a venetian blind fall back into place in the living room window. By the time he stepped out of the bus, Jessie had the front door open and called out a welcome.

She held the door open only inches until he was on the porch, then swung it wide, glancing beyond him into the woods opposite the road. She slammed the door behind Cox and nervously asked, "Did they get him yet? Has Mary been found? Have you seen Ned?"

"No, that's why I'm here. I thought you might be able to give me a tip or two. Where's Ned?" Cox asked.

"He left before dawn this morning and I haven't heard from him yet. He promised to come home for lunch and I have it all ready. You just take off your coat and sit down," she said.

"Thanks, but I'll just go back to the command post and grab something from the Salvation Army kitchen," he replied.

A wave of her hand rejected the reply. "What's the matter? Don't you like spaghetti and meatballs? Like I said, there's plenty and anyhow Ned might not get back in time to eat. Do you want me to throw all this out?" she asked with a wave toward the kitchen.

"Not on Friday the thirteenth, I don't," Cox answered when he caught the aroma. It was about to be his first real meal since Wednesday. "To hell with the kidnapper for awhile," he thought.

For more than half an hour, they talked about the kidnapping. Jessie felt that the same man who stalked her and crippled her husband was the one who kidnapped the girl.

"I just know someone is going to die before this thing is all over. I feel it in my bones. . . ." Her voice trailed away with a choke. "That poor girl," she added, almost in a whisper.

They were still seated at the kitchen table when they heard the sound of a shot. Jessie screamed as Cox automatically reached for the pistol strapped to his belt. "Christ, maybe this is it!" he exclaimed, jumping up and moving to the front doorway.

He opened the door and stepped onto the porch, his hand still resting on the gun. "Stay in there and lock the door. I'm going to see what's going on," he said over his shoulder to Jessie.

"God, be careful," she cautioned, closing the door and slamming the bolt into place behind him.

Cox stooped low as he moved to the bus and scanned the wooded area across the highway in the direction of the shot. Walking toward the highway was a uniformed state trooper, a man in a business suit, and between them, another man in a plaid shirt with his hands manacled.

The two on either side were grim, but the other, obviously their prisoner, wore a smile. His head was steady but his eyes danced in every direction as he walked toward Cox.

"You," the man in the suit directed to Cox. "That your car?" he indicated with a nod of his head toward the bus.

"Yeah. Can I help?" Cox replied, swallowing to control his excitement.

"You can take us back up the road near the command post. We left our cruiser there," he added, as the three crossed the road and stood beside the vehicle.

"Sure. Anything at all," Cox answered.

"Then open the damned door so we can get in," the plainclothesman said. The top of his bald head shone with perspiration.

Cox opened the side door, and the trooper stepped in first. He still had a grip on the smiling man's left arm. He pulled the prisoner in and the plainclothes officer, obviously over-exerted from the foot chase, followed.

"Just sit there, don't move. Don't even breathe heavy," the officer told the prisoner. The uniformed trooper had his service revolver out, lying across his lap with the barrel pointed at the midsection of the still-smiling prisoner. The plainclothesman removed his weapon and casually followed suit when he settled in place.

"Any sharp move and we're gonna have to mess up this nice man's car. You don't want that now, do you?" the plainclothesman asked. He didn't expect nor did he receive an answer. Still, the prisoner smiled. It was a strange, all-knowing smile.

"Anytime you're ready," the plainclothesman directed Cox, who still was standing outside the car, his hand on the side door.

"Sure, OK. Anything . . ." Cox trailed off, amazed that he could even speak. "Christ, don't start that all over again," the plainclothesman said.

Cox jumped into the front seat of the VW bus, cranked over the motor and swung the sharp-turning vehicle around in the narrow roadway, heading toward Shade Gap. Out of the corner of his eye he caught a glimpse of Jessie, standing in the doorway holding his coat.

"I'll be back later," he called, and waved.

Cox kept one eye on the road and the other on the smiling face that stared into the rearview mirror. The prisoner was in his thirties. Muscles rippled in his arms under the heavy shirt. He was nearly six feet tall.

"Just what the hell were you running for?" one of the officers asked the smiling man.

"'Cause I wanted to get there faster," the man replied in a voice that defied description. It was neither falsetto nor deep, but a combination of both.

"Well, I'll be damned," was the reply from the plainclothesman.

"Yeah," responded the trooper.

A half-mile east of the picnic grounds Cox was told to stop near a cruiser parked on the opposite side of the road. The motor of the cruiser was still running, although the car was empty.

Cox reached into the open glovebox for his camera. He snapped off a shot of the departing trio as they stepped out of the bus; then he leaped to the ground and took better aim before the clicking of a second and third shot.

Smiling Face grinned happily into the lens, but the two officers turned grim at the sight of the camera. They didn't even offer thanks, just pushed their prisoner into the rear seat of the cruiser and drove off.

"Hot damn, you all. I got the kidnapper in an exclusive photo with his captors. Front page banner headlines with at least a four-column shot," Cox said to himself. He jammed the bus into gear and roared up the short distance to the picnic grounds, careening into the dirt road leading to the command post. He was oblivious to the bounces as the vehicle jolted to a stop beside hundreds of other parked cars.

He rushed to the command post, clutching his camera for other shots he might be able to grab, and suddenly came to a stop at the door. A burly cop was standing, arms akimbo, in the door frame, blocking all entrance.

"What you want?" he rumbled in a deep voice.

"Only a picture of the guy just brought in here—his name, address, age and any other pertinent details available," Cox answered.

"What guy? Ain't no guy just brung in here. You crazy?"

"Bull! Don't give me that. I drove him here in my car," Cox responded with bravado nutured by growing exasperation. "Lemme talk to Mitarnowski," he continued.

"You mean the lieutenant?" the burly cop sneered.

"Yeah. That's who I want to talk to," Cox replied, wondering if that mass of muscles could move.

It wasn't quite an even staring contest. Cox was a foot shorter than the giant and weighed about half as much, but he stood firm. Amazingly enough, the giant gave ground first, turned and bellowed out to an unseen officer inside the command post to get the lieutenant. "Some smart bastard wants to talk to him here at the door."

When the giant turned around, he glared angrily at Cox. A small crowd had gathered behind Cox now, taking in the commotion.

Lieutenant Mitarnowski appeared behind the giant and took over the glaring when the giant moved aside. "Who wants to talk to me?" the lieutenant asked, scowling in turn at the gathering crowd and Cox.

"Him," the giant thumbed.

"Well," the lieutenant said, using his most irritated tone.

"All I want is the name of the guy your men just brought in," Cox mustered against the growing odds.

"I don't know what you're talking about," Mitarnowski replied indignantly. "You reporters are holding back our investigation. Why don't you go over in the shade and wait until I call you with a report of any news?"

"I've got a deadline," Cox replied. "I need some information. You've had the guy long enough to get at least a tentative identification. That's enough for now."

"You apparently didn't hear what I just said. We have no

suspect in custody. We haven't taken any suspects into custody. You're mistaken, totally wrong in your information. Now go away and don't bother us. When we want you to know something, we'll give you a release." The commander in chief of the operation disappeared into the sanctity of the building.

The giant appeared in his place.

# THE FOURTH DAY    *Saturday, May 14, 1966*

"You're a hard guy to get hold of, Mac," Charlie Griffith, chief security officer of Pennsylvania Electric Company, said into the telephone. "I've been trying to get you for hours."

It was 6:00 A.M., and he was talking to Thomas McGinn of the K-9 Academy in El Dorado, Arkansas. McGinn, along with his dogs, Weid and King, was famous for his tracking ability. Only a few years before, McGinn had made headlines in pursuing Willis Baker, who was wanted for armed robbery, jail break and assault with a deadly weapon. McGinn, with Weid and King, tracked Baker from Bisbee, Arizona, for 5 days for a total of 212 miles through some of the roughest country imaginable. When they finally brought Baker down, neither dog had pads left on its paws. All told, Weid and King had worked around the world on a total of 363 cases.

McGinn wasted no time on preliminaries. "You didn't call at this hour to chat. Just what the hell have you got in mind?" he asked.

"We got a kidnapping in the woods up here in Pennsylvania. The cops are totally baffled and the tracking dogs are in over their heads. They just can't pick up the scent and they're running in circles. I know what you and your dogs have done in the past. We know what you did at the atomic electric plant at Saxton, and I think that if you bring in your best dogs, you can wrap this thing up in no time and maybe save the girl's life," Griffith added.

McGinn sat up in bed. "Fill me in," he said.

Within minutes, Mac knew as much as his caller and was assured that the electric company would pick up the tab for the expenses. "Take a plane and get up here as fast as you can. Lieutenant Mitarnowski is the officer in charge and he has given his approval. They've spent two years on this one and the cops here are on orders to wrap this up or hunt new jobs," Charlie told Mac.

Mac thought for a minute. "The weather here is pure hell, but if I can get a plane, I'll see you in a little while. If I can't get one, I'll throw what I need in the trailer and move out as soon as I can get clearance from the owners of the academy." He put the phone back on the hook.

McGinn had no difficulty getting approval to join the hunt. After making the necessary calls he learned the weather was too dangerous for a small plane and the forecast left little hope for the next twenty-four hours.

"Hell, I can drive up there faster than that," he decided. Along with his wife, Helen, their infant daughter and King and Weid, McGinn left late Saturday afternoon for Shade Gap. He drove continuously for the next 17 hours, covering 1,260 miles, stopping only for gasoline and food.

At command headquarters, later that day, Lieutenant Mitarnowski was chewing Cox out. "The suspects we brought into the command post for questioning were just that—suspects, nothing else. As it turned out, they were innocent people who had nothing to do with the kidnapping or any of the other crimes over the past two years. We've questioned a lot of people in the valley ever since we got here," Mitarnowski admonished Cox after being presented a copy of the *Public Opinion* which showed photographs of the two suspects brought in the day before.

"All you had to do yesterday was to say they were suspects and ask us to hold off," Cox countered. "Telling us the events didn't happen was a hell of a good way to let us know you had something to hide. Trying to make the reporters here look stupid wasn't the best move," Cox continued. "We have a job to do here the same as you. Cooperation might not help a lot, but I don't think it'll hurt either."

"Look," Mitarnowski replied, "if this guy is still in the area, he probably has a radio. He'll hear anything we reveal to the news media. We can't tip our hand. Hell, he's already a jump ahead of us at every turn."

Cox shrugged his shoulders. "He knows he's a kidnapper. He knows you're after him. He knows you're questioning suspects. What in the hell difference does it make if the rest of the world knows about it? If he's in the area, he can see what's going on all around here. We don't want your secrets or plans of attack—just the official report of what everyone else can see in the open. We want the guy just as badly as you."

"You'll get all the news we feel won't hurt our investigation," Mitarnowski said, ready to break off this donnybrook with the reporter.

"OK. We'll play it your way. What did the Army helicopter deliver just now?" Cox asked.

It was Mitarnowski's turn to shrug. "What helicopter? I didn't see a helicopter." He turned and went inside the command post. Outside, the small group of newsmen stood silently with amazed looks on their faces. They had just returned from the baseball diamond where a jet helicopter had landed. The pilot handed a briefcase to an officer and roared off.

In addition to dozens of still photographs taken by reporters, one television crew was on hand to get the jet coming and going. Yet, the official report was that it hadn't happened.

Cox and Peiffer walked away, fuming over the latest rebuff. "No wonder you can pick up ten different newspapers and think you're reading about ten different kidnappings," Cox said to Peiffer, as the two made their way back to the parking lot. "But getting pissed off at the world isn't going to help solve this thing or get us a story. Let's see what those Green Berets are doing before they get away," Cox suggested, watching two young soldiers unraveling lengths of rope and climbing equipment.

"I'll grab some shots," Peiffer said, unbuckling his camera.

The men sent in from a base near Harrisburg couldn't offer any new information for the newsmen. They had been told only that they would be needed to climb down into a number of caves in the surrounding mountains. "How the hell are you going to find them?" Cox asked, out of curiosity.

"Oh, I thought you knew," the soldier said. "That chopper brought maps flown in from Washington. They brought in topographical maps from the U.S. Forest Service, the Agricultural Service, and even maps made way back in the W.P.A. days when men were sent up here to map this entire area. There's not a two-foot depression in these mountains that hasn't been located. According to the guys in charge here, they think the victim—what's her name?—is dead and her body stuffed down one of the caves."

"Bless you, sir, for talking to us," Cox told the soldier.

As Cox and Peiffer moved away from the soldiers, Cox commented, "Now I know why Mitarnowski didn't want to reveal the helicopter incident. Makes sense if the kidnapper is still in the hills and armed with a radio. But he still could have made his point in a different way."

"Think I'll tag along with the Green Berets till dark," Peiffer said. "I'll find one of the police we know in the area and pick his brain," Cox replied.

After a short search, Cox spotted Sergeant Hoover devouring a hot dog at the Salvation Army kitchen.

"Quit bugging the lieutenant or you'll wind up on the FBI and State Police Most Wanted List," the officer suggested to his friend.

"He bugs the hell outta me," Cox replied. Then Cox told Hoover why the Army helicopter had arrived and what was in the briefcase delivered to the command post.

"You going to use it?" Hoover asked.

"Hell, no. You know me better than that, I hope. If the son-of-a-bitch is still in the area and has a radio, he could easily dump tons of rock down on a cave and make it impossible for anyone to find Mary's body, if she's already dead," Cox said.

"The reason Mitarnowski can't tell everything he knows is that he can't trust any of the newsmen. He doesn't know any of them and can't reveal any 'hot' information for fear one gung-ho bastard would use it. Give him a break. He's doing the right thing under the circumstances," Hoover pleaded.

"OK. But I still don't have to like the guy," Cox answered.

"Say. Did you ever hear anything about a local yokel named 'Bicycle Pete'?" Hoover asked.

"It seems as though someone like that was mentioned when I was up here on earlier attacks. Why do you ask?" Cox queried, attempting to hide his interest.

"Well, there's this guy who has been missing from his home down toward Burnt Cabins since the kidnapping. Hollenbaugh, Hollyburger, something like that. We're checking him out now. Seems like he goes off without telling anyone. A sort of recluse, no friends, just a couple of dogs or something like that. They say he rides a bicycle all over these back roads up here and never looks up to see where he's going. Sort of a weirdo. Guess there's at least one in every community," Hoover added.

"Can't recall where I heard of him before, but I think I've seen him riding that damn bike around when I was up here last year. You're not planning to put an all-points out for the guy with a young girl on a bike, accompanied with two or three dogs, are you?" Cox asked jokingly.

"Naw, not yet. I'll let you know if we do," Hoover said, laughing as he walked toward the command post, waving one hand in parting.

# THE FIFTH DAY   *Sunday, May 15, 1966*

McGinn, despite his weariness from more than seventeen hours behind the wheel, arrived at the command post shortly before dawn on Sunday. He secured accommodations for his wife and child in a motel at Fort Littleton.

Minutes later he passed countless police, civilian, and military cars as he drove through the Shade Gap picnic grounds toward his meeting with the officials in charge.

Sergeant Kimmel, alerted that the tracker had arrived, met Mac as he parked near the command post.

"Looks like a war going on here," Mac said in greeting Kimmel.

"Believe me, it's nothing short of it. Our biggest hope now is that we get the guy before someone in that mob out there finds him," the sergeant said.

"Damned if I ever remember this part of Pennsylvania being so rugged. I can see how you couldn't find a guy hiding here unless he was flushed out," Mac said, as the two walked toward the meeting with Mitarnowski and FBI agent Joe Jamieson.

Inside, the thoroughness of the organization struck Mac.

He noted the separate provisions of the state police and the FBI. Though it was only daybreak, more than two dozen men were already at work, poring over maps and records.

Once the introductions had been made, Mac was briefed by Mitarnowski and Jamieson on the developments to date.

"What we need to know is this: can your dogs follow a cold trail?" Jamieson asked.

"My dogs are cold trackers," Mac answered. "When a trail is only a couple of hours old, a bloodhound is the best bet. Weid and King pick up the scent from the air, not the ground. If the guy is still in the area, we'll find him," he assured Jamieson.

"That's the best news I heard since we got here," Jamieson answered. Mitarnowski agreed, adding that neither the bloodhound nor the four state police tracking dogs had had any luck. "They were running around in circles. This guy is smart and apparently knows dogs well enough to be able to throw them off the scent. Grab a bite to eat, then we'll get started. No sense letting the trail get any colder," Mitarnowski added.

While Mac was eating breakfast, Trooper George Plafcan, of the Huntingdon substation, and Dave Walker, of the FBI's Philadelphia office, took seats on either side of him. "We're assigned to assist you with the dogs," Plafcan said, introducing himself and his companion. Both men had worked with dogs before. "Our first chore is to find the girl's body. Or at least look for it somewhere to the west of here." He looked embarrassed. "Seems there's a clairvoyant who claims to have seen a vision of the girl's body as well as the kidnapper's hideout. We gotta check it out," he said, expecting a laugh. He didn't get it. Mac had gone on dozens of hunts based on similar information.

"Let's go. I'm ready as I'll ever be," he said, moving in the direction of his dogs.

"Let's go up to the command post again. We can prime the dogs with the scent of the girl as well as the scent of our chief suspect at this time," Walker directed. "Didn't know we have a chief suspect," Mac countered.

"Yes. A recluse who lives down by Burnt Cabins. He's got a record as a criminal as well as a history of mental illness. Name's Hollenbaugh," Jamieson answered.

Within thirty minutes, Weid had been given the scent of Mary Lou from clothing kept in a plastic bag and King was taken to the Hollenbaugh cabin and primed with scent from bed clothing. The dogs were ready.

The clairvoyant was taken along on the hunt. He directed the men to an open field three miles southeast of the command post and pointed out a rock pile. "Her body's under there," he announced proudly.

Within ten minutes, however, Weid ruled out the vision. The clairvoyant was obviously shattered. "It was so real. I really saw her. And I saw the kidnapper, holed up in the mountains there," he said, pointing in the direction of the Tuscarora.

Walker dropped the clairvoyant off at the picnic grounds and watched the dejected man walk away through the maze of parked cars.

"There's no mistake. She just isn't there," Mac told Plafcan. "Weid's found men buried under a twelve-foot avalanche. He just doesn't make a mistake like that." The idea of moving the entire rock pile by bulldozer was abandoned.

The three men then took the dogs to Dry Run Hollow, the point where the bloodhound had led a posse in circles. By noon, it was obvious that neither dog had picked up any scent—Mary Lou's or the kidnapper's. The search was abandoned and the trio returned to the command post.

After lunch, maps of the area revealed the location of eight caves in the Black Log Mountain, west of Shade Gap. "Check out every one of the caves, but this time we're sending along some reinforcements," Jamieson said. "If this guy is the same man who has shot up the area for the past two years, he can hit anything he aims at. We're taking no chances."

The search party swelled to twelve agents and state policemen, who trudged along behind the dogs as they wove a path four miles into the woods. By midafternoon, the men and dogs located seven of the caves, some of which were barely large enough for a man to stand, or for two people to sleep.

The eighth cave, however, high over the valley, proved to be the first real clue to the whereabouts of the victim. And it was the first positive identification of the kidnapper. King's actions showed beyond a doubt that William Diller Hollenbaugh had been in the cave. Weid's similar discovery indicated that at the same time Mary Lou had been there—at the most, two days before.

The opening to the cave was small and the men had to crawl to reach the larger area which was about eight feet long. The cave was damp, but the scent had lingered. There was no sign that the kidnapper and his victim had been there, but the numerous bottomless pits that fell away inside the enclosure could have swallowed up anything, forever.

When the dogs were taken outside the cave to continue the hunt, they lost the scent entirely and were unable to point the hunters in a direction their quarry had taken.

Even with the latest setback, the men were exuberant when they returned to the command post that afternoon. Their elusive quarry was now a known quantity.

Mac was feeding his dogs when FBI agent Terry Anderson approached.

"They're beautiful dogs," Anderson said, "and you should be proud of them. I heard what they did earlier this afternoon."

"Thanks. But I wouldn't get too close," Mac cautioned. "They don't take too kindly to strangers."

"They look friendly enough," a second agent said, reaching out to pat Weid on the head. In a split second the dog lunged. A short leash and a quick response from the agent saved his hand from being severed at the wrist. He left without further comment.

"I like dogs. Have a setter of my own. I think Weid is beautiful," Anderson said again.

Then Anderson reached out and patted Weid on the head. This time the dog only whimpered. "Looks like you got a friend," Mac said, bewildered.

"A friend," Anderson repeated.

Later, when the rapport was made known to Jamieson, Anderson was assigned to accompany Mac and the dogs in the search.

Since Wednesday, gray skies had dominated the daylight hours of Shade Gap, adding nothing to the drooping spirit of the residents. But today, at mid-morning, the weather was perfect.

From the focal point—the police command post—more than 600 civilians, 100 state police and nearly two dozen FBI agents, along with a small army of newsmen, moved out across the valley. The four-mile perimeter which had been trampled over and over was widened to mountain ranges on the east and west, and as far south as Burnt Cabins.

Every occupied residence was revisited, every uninhabited building searched with or without the owner's permission and knowledge. Logging trails and deer paths, now bare of game animals, were trod for the first time in years.

Cox and Peiffer, after following one group of police and volunteers into the deep woods west of Shade Gap off the dirt Mountain Foot Road, returned to the command post and decided to sit this one out. They had hopes of getting some information from the many police still there, on future plans. One of the more intriguing developments they picked up was the fact the police now thought that Mary Lou was still alive.

Cox noticed that troopers were carrying rifles in their hands rather than strapped to their shoulders as they did only yesterday. Most of the troopers were using binoculars freely now, scanning the distant hills carefully before they moved ahead. There were other peculiar differences. The police were less vocal than before, cautioning the men in the posse to keep their voices low. The groups were more spread out than before. There was daylight between the searchers today, where Saturday, the same men were ordered to stick together and direct their eyes to the ground for clues. Today, the orders were to search ahead for any reflected light, any movement in the distance.

The civilians in the group were ordered, both at the command post before they began their search and again before the party gathered to cross the open fields, to remain behind the lines established by police, and not to shoot for any reason without express directions from an officer in charge.

"Ken, tell you what. You find someone in the area who knows where this 'Bicycle Pete'—or whoever he is—lives. It's not much to go on, but it's better than anything we've had yet. Maybe you can con someone into taking you to his house and giving you a little background.

"I'll get something on the guy from Arkansas, this tracker, and grab some pictures for the paper tomorrow. If McGinn and his dogs are anything like the rumors flying around here, we'll be getting some action soon," Cox said.

"Sounds like the best bet yet. Even if Hollenbaugh's innocent, at least it will add color to the story—something we're beginning to need. How long do you think you can go on filling the wires with rehash?" Peiffer asked.

"I'm about burned out now. Get going. I'll meet you back here this afternoon." Cox moved toward a spot under the trees where he had seen two big dogs being fed a short time ago.

McGinn, who until now had shied away from the newsmen, confided in Cox that he was using the scent of Mary Lou's clothing, and other clothing taken from the cabin of a prime suspect near Burnt Cabins.

"We're going up into the hills later today to search some more caves where the kidnapper might have taken the girl," he told the newsman. He paused. "Sorry, no civilians are going along, but come back this evening and I'll let you know how we made out."

"See you here at suppertime, and thanks a hell of a lot. If you don't feel up to repeating the story to other newsmen, I won't be a damn bit mad." Cox was hoping for a scoop.

"You're the first newsman I talked to yet, and I'm not going out of my way to dig them up," McGinn said, waving as Cox left.

Ned Price agreed to show Peiffer where Hollenbaugh lived. But Price gave little credence to the notion that Hollenbaugh was the kidnapper. "He's just a little guy. The bastard who shot me was over six feet tall," Ned said.

When Peiffer and Price arrived at the small cabin along Route 522, two police officers were seated in a cruiser at the driveway. While they offered no objection to Peiffer and Price moving onto the property, it was obvious they were uneasy.

Neither policeman offered any new information, saying only that they were assigned to keep a lookout around the cabin and to talk to the guy who lived there when he showed up. The impression they gave was that it was a waste of time, and that they could be serving the hunt better if they would be allowed to join the rest of the groups on a track into the woods.

Gary Willhide, cub reporter from the *Public Opinion*, given the first opportunity to join the manhunt, was sidetracked when the editor learned of church services planned for Mary Lou. He was directed to cover the event—an emotional prayer service at the Pleasant Hill Evangelical United Brethren Church, a half mile from the Broderick home.

"Shall we gather around the altar and pray for Mary's safe return?" the Reverend Raymond A. Piper, pastor of the Shade Gap area charge, asked.

The congregation, numbering about fifty women and children, filed slowly to the front of the sanctuary.

The warm sun sifted through the colored-glass windows as the pastor led the parishioners in prayer.

Tearfully, Mary's friends, neighbors and classmates prayed on their knees for her return. With equal earnestness, they prayed for the Christian salvation of her abductor, the mysterious Mountain Man.

Later that afternoon, McGinn, accompanied by FBI agent Terry Anderson, fed Weid and King while discussing the afternoon search with Cox, Peiffer and Willhide. The newsmen had met Anderson several years before.

"We found some evidence the girl was taken to a cave in the mountains west of here recently, but don't know just when. The dogs picked up her scent in one of the caves, but it could have been as long ago as Wednesday night," McGinn said. "Once outside the cave, the dogs lost the scent. It would have lingered in the cave because it was protected from the elements."

Agent Anderson took up the story. "We can't give you any more than that now. Try to understand our situation. The kidnapper is probably equipped with a radio and is getting every bit of news that leaks out. We honestly can't give you any more info than that." His tone was apologetic, but at the same time he was obviously calling a halt to further questioning.

Cox noticed that Anderson was favoring his right shoulder and frequently rubbing it with his left hand. "Did you hurt yourself up there?" the reporter asked.

"No. It's just my bursitis acting up. Always does in this kind of weather and I've been wet more than I've been dry these past couple of days. Maybe I'll get a chance to get home tomorrow and get something to fix it up," he said.

"Well, take care. We'll see you later," Cox said, before turning away from the men.

As the three newsmen made their way to the Salvation Army kitchen, Cox said, "I think we'd better keep a close track on McGinn. His dogs have accomplished more in one day than the police and other dogs did since Wednesday. I got a feeling he's where the action is."

"Or will be," Willhide added.

"It never ceases to amaze me how the cops keep so much hidden. You know damn well there was more discovered up there than just an old scent of Mary Lou. There's just no way on earth that cops could become reporters," Peiffer added.

The trio changed direction just then as crowds began to surge toward the command post. They fell in line and moved close to the door of the metal building as Lieutenant Mitarnowski emerged.

"I have a statement to make to all of you," he began, "and afterward I want members of the news media to pick up an artist's sketch of the kidnapper. It was drawn from descriptions given by the Broderick children. But first, I want to announce that we are today abandoning the massive inch-by-inch search of the area by all the volunteers. We are not abandoning the hunt. It will not be abandoned until the kidnapper has been apprehended and Mary Lou has been found.

"But we know that many of you—students and those who work for a living—must return to school and to your jobs. Some of you have been here since we started and have done your very best, but we cannot ask you to continue as we must. Go back to school and your jobs. We'll carry on from now.

"But remember, the hunt will continue until Mary is found and her abductor is brought to justice. In addition to state police and FBI agents, professional men such as foresters and game protectors will continue the search. We're not giving up."

Lieutenant Mitarnowski scanned the crowd. "Just to bring you up to date, we have no progress to report, either on Mary or the kidnapper. We are checking leads sent in by well-meaning people, but have not turned up a concrete suspect.

"We feel that the kidnapper is a resident of the area,

however, and we are keeping an open mind on any suspects," he concluded.

He looked at the three newsmen. "Now if you gentlemen from the press will come to the door of the command post, we'll give you a copy of the police artist's work." He returned to the building. The several hundred men who had gathered to hear the announcement dispersed slowly, grumbling that the police were giving up, regardless of the assurance to the contrary.

The artist's drawing showed a man wearing a baseball cap, goggle-type glasses and khaki clothing. He was thin, with irregular front teeth and purported to be about five feet, nine inches tall.

"What do you think?" Willhide asked Cox and Peiffer.

"I think the cops are getting closer, and they want the civilians out of the way before the fireworks begin," said Cox.

"Me too," Peiffer answered. "This is the first time I ever heard a cop worrying whether a civilian shows up for work or not, or a kid gets back to school. Something just doesn't ring true."

"Well, let's go back and tell the world about it," Willhide suggested.

"Just for the hell of it, let's drive by the Broderick home on the way home," Bob suggested.

With twilight rapidly approaching, the trio drove down the narrow dirt road past the Brodericks' house, pulling off to the side dozens of times over the two mile distance to allow other vehicles to pass in the opposite direction. Most were filled with men, women and children who paid far more attention to the surrounding area than to the road.

"Did you see some of the license plates? I'll bet there are more out-of-state cars here than local ones. Ohio, Maryland, West Virginia, New Jersey. God, I can't remember all the states," Willhide commented. Traffic was nearly bumper to bumper on the normally desolate road.

"Look there! I can't believe what I see," Peiffer chimed in as the vehicle approached the home of the kidnap victim.

Dozens of children were playing football on a field adjacent to the Broderick home, while curious sightseers peered at the home itself. Cars were parked halfway onto the road, nearly blocking passage. It had turned into a circus.

# THE SIXTH DAY  *Monday, May 16,1966*

When Cox arrived at Shade Gap the next morning at seven, Peiffer was already there—and complaining. "I've had more damn cops ask me who 'Bicycle Pete' is since you blew the cover in the paper. I've been here a half hour and every one of them thinks we know more than they do," he began. "Not only that, some of them are pissed, thinking they should know at least as much as some 'yokel reporter.' One cop told me that when he asked the powers-that-be who you were talking about, he got cut off."

"What did you tell them?" Cox asked, grinning mischievously.

"If they want anything, they get it from you," Peiffer answered, obviously unprepared to meet the onslaught that early in the morning.

"Hell, far as I'm concerned, tell 'em what we know," Cox answered. "After all, I only said the investigators were looking for the guy to answer some questions. I didn't say he was the guilty party; just that he was missing, that's all."

Sergeant Hoover gave Cox the first hint that the higher-ups were looking for a clue to the leak.

"Hi, Les. How's tricks?" Cox asked the officer when he moved beside him in the coffee line.

Hoover turned, winked quickly and said, "See you got the thing solved. Nice work. Gotta get back to the post. See you later," the words rushed out of his mouth. He turned quickly and walked toward the large metal building.

"Hope he didn't get into trouble because he knows us," Peiffer said.

"No way. He's a vet with the greatest poker face in the world. He could lie his way out of hell and get a halo for doing it," Cox answered.

Just then a heavy hand clamped on his shoulder. He turned and looked up into the face of Gus Alexiou. "Bring your coffee over to our table voluntarily or we slap you with a warrant," Alexiou demanded with a straight face. He pointed to a bench occupied by some of the officers from the Chambersburg and McConnellsburg substations, all familiar faces.

"Sure, just as soon as I get my arm in a sling and my shoulder in a cast," Cox replied.

"All we need to do now is make sure we sit upwind. The shit's going to hit the fan," Peiffer offered.

"Forget it. We've been thrown out of better dumps than this," Cox answered bravely, thankful that the inquisition was in friendly quarters.

"Give," was the order from Alexiou as the pair joined the small group of police.

"Nothing to give. You saw it all in the paper," Cox replied, hiding behind a cup of steaming coffee.

"Bull. You know something. You got the general all excited. Give," Alexiou repeated.

"Well, it's like this. You know how my love life has been suffering from living in this paradise for the past week. Well, I merely put my genius to work to solve ..." He couldn't finish.

"Crap. Don't break your other arm patting yourself on the back just because you've become good buddies with the locals here. All we want are the facts," Rocky Rockwell interrupted, sounding like something out of "Dragnet."

"Since you put it that way, the truth is that Bicycle Pete has been missing from his shack down the road toward Burnt Cabins since Mary Lou was kidnapped. And he matches somewhat the artist's conception of the guy who kidnapped her. You know, that drawing made up from the description given by Mary's brothers and sisters."

Cox went on. "Some of your men have had a stakeout at the place since late Saturday and all day Sunday. But the report I get is that this joker came back to his shack to feed his dogs right under the noses of your boys and they never saw him. Other than that, you know as much as we do," Cox concluded.

"You must have hit a nerve," Trooper Swider said. "The heads of state are checking on this guy—Hollenbaugh—harder than hell since your article. If I were you, I wouldn't be too disappointed if Mitarnowski and Jamieson don't roll out the red carpet when they see you," he continued.

"If I had to depend on them for news, you wouldn't believe the white space we'd have on page one," Cox answered. "Wasn't anything I said that's not gospel. And if any of you guys have to report back to the generals, tell them there's no use looking for a leak. What we have, we got on our own. Another thing—no way would I reveal a source anyhow. Before I'd do that, I'd throw in my typewriter," he offered, hoping for any tidbit that might be forthcoming. But none was; the inquisition was over.

"When you pick this guy up to hand him over to us, let me know. I'd like to be able to tell my wife something that she doesn't have to wait to read in the paper," Alexiou said, unwinding his lanky legs from under the picnic table. The other officers followed suit, leaving for the command post and new assignments or to make a report to their superiors.

"See, that wasn't so bad," Cox said to Peiffer when they were alone at the table again.

"Not as bad as I thought, but I'll bet we can't get the time of day from anyone else in the know here," Peiffer replied.

Terry Anderson sat on the platform that separated the FBI

section from the state police in the command post. Thoughtfully, he watched the faces of the men around him, while he waited for his long-distance call to be completed. Most of the forty state policemen and twenty-one FBI agents still on the job were milling about in the building, enjoying the lunch break.

A half-dozen were on the telephone, nodding at the answers to their questions. Every scrap of information was recorded on scratch pads.

Anderson's mind was racing over the hundreds of calls that had come in from well-meaning persons, when Margie answered the phone.

He snapped back to reality at the sound of her voice. "Hi, hon. Just wanted to let you know I'll be home tonight. The reason I'm calling, in addition to hearing your voice, is to ask you to pack some things for me. You know, some clean underclothes and socks. And by the way, put in a flask of whiskey and some adhesive tape. My bursitis is raising hell and I need the warmth and comfort of a nurse. You're the first one that came to mind," he said.

"And I better be the last one too," Margie answered threateningly.

"Love you. See you tonight," Anderson concluded.

Agent Tom Dolan, whom Anderson had replaced when the FBI got its first call, joked, "Margie isn't going to try to sue Jamieson for alienation of affections, is she?"

"Hope not. My old aching body just couldn't stand a scandal," the agent answered, kneading the flesh on his right shoulder.

He had been aloft that morning—his first ride in a helicopter. The craft searched the area of the caves discovered on Sunday. The cold blast from the rotor blades affected his bursitis. He needed a rest. But that would have to wait. Anderson was scheduled to go out that afternoon with McGinn and his tracking dogs, Weid and King. Their destination was the Hollenbaugh cabin.

Within an hour, Anderson, McGinn and two state policemen felt the same excitement Weid and King exhibited at the cabin. The dogs were on a hot trail, straining at their leashes. The trail pointed west into the deep woods.

Using his two-way radio, Anderson informed Jamieson that the dogs had picked up scents from Hollenbaugh and the girl. "According to Mac, the trail is only a couple of hours old."

"Have your guards fan out beside you. Keep some daylight between you whenever you can, and I'll send in a chopper!" Jamieson told the agent.

Winding along behind the dogs, the men traveled about four miles to a point high atop a knoll west of Hollenbaugh's cabin. Just below the searchers, the Mountain Foot Road twisted through the valley.

Holding onto the killer dogs was nearly impossible when the search party approached an abandoned car at an old logging trail.

"We're close, damn close," Mac informed them.

"OK. We'll wait here for reinforcements," the agent ordered, noting the approach of the helicopter from the east. Using his portable radio, he directed the pilot to their location. Two more agents joined the chase and the pilot was instructed to fly south, in an attempt to throw off the quarry if he was in the vicinity.

"Four troopers are coming in to join us from the road below. They should be here soon," one of the newly arrived agents said. Within five minutes, they appeared from the scrub, attesting to the ability of a man to hide in the thick underbrush.

The ten-man search party fanned out behind the dogs and the hunt continued. Several hundred yards south, the dogs lost the trail completely.

"That bastard. He must be using mace to kill the scent. He can't be more than a couple miles away, but we've lost him completely," McGinn said through clenched teeth. They stood there watching the dogs circle the immediate area in frustration.

"We'll move on down the ridge and start a new sweep. Maybe the dogs can pick up a fresh scent,' McGinn suggested.

"Well, we have nothing to lose now," Terry agreed as the posse moved out.

An hour later the search was abandoned when a radio message from the state police directed the posse south along the Mountain Foot Road. Another search party had discovered items stolen earlier from a cabin. Behind the buildings, deep in the woods, canned goods, a quart of whiskey, candy, a gun holster, various items of men's and women's clothing, kitchen utensils, hunting knives and other objects were found wrapped in a sheet buried under a large pile of wood pulp and covered with leaves.

Rain had washed off the leaves, leaving the white sheet exposed. It was discovered by a trooper when the police were called to investigate the burglary.

"They planned to come back here again," Anderson offered, counting in the discovery cosmetics and men's and women's toilet articles.

"The trail is cold now, but I think Weid and King can pick it up again if we give them time," Mac said, studying his animals.

"The owner said the stuff was taken a couple of days ago. He was here Friday and the place hadn't been burglarized then," Anderson replied.

"Doesn't matter, the dogs have the trail, I'm sure. We still have enough daylight left," McGinn said.

"Let's go then," the agent answered, directing the posse to follow.

The dogs, obviously on the scent of the victim and her abductor, lost it again after two miles of travel toward the knoll they had just searched. Again, the trail was lost at a small mountain stream.

With darkness approaching, the search was called off and the group returned to the command post to study maps sent in from Washington. Photographs of Hollenbaugh had been flown in that afternoon from the state mental institution at

Waymart and they, too, would be studied with great interest.

It was getting on toward midnight when Terry Anderson began the drive home. He caught the Turnpike at Fort Littleton and headed the cruiser towards Camp Hill. The hour-long drive gave him time to consider the case and the prime suspect, Hollenbaugh. The information he now had was more than enough for Anderson to decide that Hollenbaugh was the kidnapper.

Hollenbaugh had been convicted in 1939, at eighteen, on burglary and larceny charges and was sentenced to a term of five to ten years in Western Penitentiary. He was later sent to Rockview and escaped, but was picked up soon after and returned to prison.

Later, in 1946, he was committed to Farview Hospital for the criminally insane. After his discharge in June, 1959, he settled in Shade Gap.

He had an eighth-grade education and was considered a scavenger. He held odd jobs in the area, but most of the money he had came from state welfare subsistence.

His "book" read that he engaged in criminal activity to gain prestige and derived satisfaction from attempting to baffle police.

"God, I wish we'd had his dossier last week. Someone, somewhere, along the chain of command goofed," Anderson said to himself.

His Irish setter, Red, announced Anderson's arrival as the cruiser stopped in the driveway of the suburban home. Margie opened the front door and the dog had his front paws on the car window before Terry could open the door.

Terry's three children, Ann, Mark and Michael, still at home, had waited up for their father. They fired a thousand questions about the past five days and got answers to all, but he would not tell them who he thought was the kidnapper, and when he would be home to stay.

It was long after midnight when he finally sent them to bed. He was glad, in a way, that his oldest, Marlynn, nineteen, was at Bloomsburg State College. He could be alone with Margie. He needed her company more than he ever could remember.

Margie told him about her recognition tea at Holy Spirit Hospital, and wanted to show him the pin she was given. But he held her tight.

"I know it's nice, but I'll see it later. Stay here beside me now. I've got to leave again in a couple of hours.

"I didn't want to say anything in front of the kids, but I think we know who we're looking for. I've got a snapshot of him in my briefcase. His name's William Hollenbaugh and he has a record and a history of mental illness which could have easily led him to this. And, he's missing.

"On top of all that, this guy's scent has been picked up along with the girl's and according to the trainer who owns the tracking dogs, they're traveling together. We tracked them yesterday from Hollenbaugh's cabin into the deep woods. Later the dogs picked up both scents at a home that was burglarized.

"Sunday, the dogs found old scents at a cave high on a mountain west of Shade Gap.

"The way McGinn's dogs have been following the trail, we should be able to finish this thing today or tomorrow at least. It won't be long now," he predicted.

"What about the girl?" she asked.

"Well, she's still alive, at least as of yesterday. And we think that if she lived this long, she's got a chance. What kind of trouble we'll get into when we trap him I don't know. I just hope he has enough sanity left to give up without a fight. I don't want to see anyone else suffer.

"God, you have to see these people to realize what they've gone through. They sure have what it takes. The guy who had his leg shot off, Price, he's on the job as much as anyone else. The husbands of the other victims are too. And the rest of the people in the valley are as determined to rid themselves of this guy as any of the victims. I only hope we can get to him before they do, or there won't be enough left to shovel up.

"I'm sorry I ever laughed at the first stories I heard coming out of the area. These people are first class. There isn't anything you ask that isn't done immediately, regardless of what it is. And they band together like nothing I ever dreamed of. What they've done is unbelievable, yet when you try to compliment them, they actually get embarrassed.

"They're all that way though. They don't have much. Actually, it's a depressed area, but what they have is yours for the asking and they apologize for not having more to give. We ask for volunteers and hundreds respond. No one wants anything; they all just want to help.

"It's a good feeling just to meet people like that," he said.

At 6:30 in the morning, they awoke to the alarm and he dressed while she made his breakfast.

After he showered and sat down at the table, Margie reminded him she would be painting at the apartment they had bought as an investment. She would be listening to the radio for late reports, she told him.

"You be careful. Stay off the ladders. Let me do that. I don't want to come back to a crippled woman," he cautioned.

"I'll be careful if you are," she responded.

"It's a deal," he answered.

Before he left for the hour's drive back, he did something he had never done before. He went into each bedroom and kissed his sleeping children.

# THE SEVENTH DAY *Tuesday, May 17, 1966*

It was 6:00 A.M. when FBI agent Edwin Greenwald yawned, rubbed his eyes and blinked into the rising sun peeking over the Tuscarora Mountains. There was only the hint of yesterday's clouds in the east. He leaned across the rear seat of the police cruiser and peered out the window to the west. The skies were perfectly clear.

State Police Captain Raymond Anderson also sat up slowly in the front seat. "Jeez, my left arm's asleep. It feels like it's missing," Ray said, rubbing his arm.

"My legs feel almost as bad. I'm going to get out and stretch," Greenwald replied. He swung open the rear door. "Gotta be a better way to make a living," he said when he discovered that he could barely stand. He had begun doing knee bends to get the circulation moving in his legs when he saw movement at the Hollenbaugh cabin, about 100 feet from the front of the cruiser.

"Ray, get your gun. There's someone or something in back of the cabin," Greenwald whispered, reaching into the back seat for his own gun.

The state policeman didn't answer. He pushed the driver's door open and hit the gravel driveway in one motion, gun in hand.

"You take the right side and I'll go around on the other side," Greenwald directed, checking his gun as he moved out of the car again.

The men separated and sprinted for the cabin, which had been under observation for the past twelve hours. They reached the back of the cabin together, and discovered a small tan dog, circling his pen, trying to get inside.

Crouching, Greenwald whistled for the dog. It responded immediately and came directly to the agent, tail wagging. The agent cradled the dog in his arm and motioned for Ray to move toward the pen.

Ray ran in a crouch just beyond the pen. For several moments, his eyes scanned the woods to the west before he turned back to his companion.

"Nothing moving out there as far as I can see. There's some ground fog in the valley, but I can't be sure," Ray said in a low voice when he returned to Greenwald, who still clutched the little dog to his side.

"I'll put this dog in the cruiser and then we'd better make a search of the cabin together," the agent said, running toward the vehicle. He placed the dog on the rear seat, closed the door and ran back to the cabin.

"I'll take the back door. You go in through the front," the state policeman directed, as he leaned against the side of the frame cabin.

"It'll take a second," Greenwald answered, quickly turning the corner of the building.

They kicked open the door simultaneously, and peered into the darkened interior. Sunlight had begun to illuminate the kitchen, but the bedroom was still as they pushed forward. Guns poked into the room first, but their precaution was unnecessary. The cabin was empty, just as it had been when they checked the night before.

"OK. Let's close it up and get back to the car and look at that mutt. It probably came back during the night. Hollenbaugh and his other dogs can't be too far away," Greenwald said.

Rather than reveal their discovery over the car radio, they decided to wait for their replacement, and then would report their find to command headquarters. Over an hour passed before the other cruiser pulled in behind them to continue the vigil.

The pair drove recklessly to the picnic grounds, four miles to the north, handed over the dog to Detective Tom Homan, and gave their report.

Agent Terry Anderson had just returned from his home and was elated at the find. "This could be it. Someone get McGinn out of the sack and over here on the double. We gotta see if his dogs can backtrack this mutt," he directed.

McGinn arrived less than fifteen minutes later and met Terry Anderson and several other agents at the pavilion where they were eating breakfast. McGinn joined them at the table where plans for the morning hunt were discussed.

"Sure, we can backtrack the dog. I'll finish this coffee and prime the dogs with the scent and we'll be on our way," McGinn said, picking up on the growing excitement in the group.

"Finish your breakfast first. While you're eating, I'll get some other men to go along with us," the agent told McGinn. Anderson moved swiftly to the command post and disappeared inside.

Joe Jamieson and Mitarnowski agreed the break was the best yet, and directed Trooper George Plafcan, Trooper Jack Stroud, and Agent Tom Dolan to accompany Anderson and McGinn. Richard Stoud, another dog handler with his dog, Apache, was also directed to go along on the hunt.

"Be damn careful," Jamieson told the men. "This guy can shoot, and you know what he's done already," referring to Price, Blake, Yohn and the others. "God knows what he'll do if he's cornered," he added.

"We'll be careful and we'll keep in touch by radio. We're getting a man to come over and identify the dog. We aren't leaving anything to chance this time," Anderson assured him.


Margie Anderson was waiting just inside the front door of her home for the arrival of a taxi. She had decided to take a cab rather than drive into the city in the eight o'clock rush hour.

She looked out of the rear window of the cab as it swung around a corner. In the distance was the faint silhouette of the Tuscarora Mountains. Terry was out there somewhere, doing the work he loved.

"He'll be home the day after tomorrow," she thought to herself. He had a speaking engagement in Carlisle on Thursday, and the Bureau made sure that when you made a promise, you kept it.

The cab driver, noticing Margie's interest in the west, asked "You hear about the kidnapping over in Shade Gap."

"Yes," she replied.

"That must be something. I have a girl that age, and I sure feel sorry for the victim and her family," the driver said.


Ken Peiffer left the darkroom at the *Public Opinion* and was going over some photographs with Bob Cox when he was called to the telephone. He noted the time: 8:15 A.M.

"Take a message and tell them to call back later. We've got to get this layout ready," Peiffer told the switchboard operator.

She spoke into the telephone for a few seconds and then called out, "They said it's important."

"Damn, I'll be right back," he told Cox and walked across the newsroom to his desk.

"I'm on my way. Thanks," he said into the phone, then hung up. "I've just got a tip from the Chambersburg Police that one of the dogs belonging to Hollenbaugh has been located and they're planning to backtrack it. Can you finish the captions from my notes?" he asked Cox.

"Yeah. Get going and call as soon as you hear something. I'll be here another hour at least," Cox replied.

"When you leave, bring me a sandwich and a Coke," Peiffer said, putting on his coat and jamming photographic equipment into his camera case. He sprinted out the back door and onto the parking lot to his car.

Cox walked over to the editor, Frank Young, and told him about the dog.

"OK. Get the story and captions written and take off," Young directed without looking up.

"How about this election stuff? You want me to finish it or give it to Gary Willhide?" Cox asked.

"That's right! Damn! Willhide's out making the rounds and won't have time when he gets back." Young thought for a moment and said, "Hell, you finish it, but keep it tight."

Cox's stomach was in knots and the thought of staying there another half-hour to write election stories did little to ease the tension. Forty minutes later he finished the Shade Gap story he had written from yesterday's notes and dropped it on the editor's desk. Then he began the tedious election account. It was one of those stories which, if time permitted, could have been meaty. Milton Shapp was challenging the Philadelphia machine. It was a hotly contested gubernational primary fight. The polls had been open for two hours, but he had little heart for it now.

Peiffer glanced down at the speedometer and found it at 75 MPH. He was glad to see the early morning traffic into the depot had cleared. The road ahead was wide open.

Peiffer rolled into the command post and spotted a possible source for a lead seated at one of the picnic tables sipping coffee. "Hey, Kissner. What's going on with the dog they found?" Peiffer asked.

Rocky Rockwell was with him, putting away another sandwich. "Can't give any secrets like that away, but if you happen to be in the vicinity of Hollenbaugh's cabin in a couple of minutes, it wouldn't hurt to have your camera along," Rockwell said.

"Thanks. That's cooperation. Now where's the nearest phone?" Peiffer asked. "I have to call Cox and tell him where to meet me."

"There's a public phone down by the gate. But if Cox hasn't left Chambersburg yet, tell him to stay home; he'll be too late," Rocky added. But Peiffer had already left.

Trooper Jack Stroud and Tom Dolan were the first to arrive at the Hollenbaugh cabin, around nine, with the small dog. They left the car and were placing the dog in his pen when they noticed that several of the dog's toes were missing on the left paw. Brief comments were exchanged and the two men walked back to the cruiser. The other men had not yet arrived.

Just then a call came in over the radio: "Take Tom Dolan with you and go to the farm down the road—the Fogal place—and bring Fogal back to identify the dog," the voice from the command post directed.

Stroud lifted the mike from the radio. "Ten-four," he replied, then placed the mike back on its keeper.

"Doubt if there are too many little tan dogs around here with toes missing on the left front paw," Dolan commented. Trooper Stroud started the car and headed for the Fogal farm.

As the cruiser moved onto the macadam road, another cruiser pulled in at the Hollenbaugh cabin. Terry Anderson braked to a stop and commented to Plafcan, "Wonder where they're going?" The FBI frequency did not carry the state police calls. A check with the FBI post, however, revealed the mission.

Anderson and Plafcan were directed to wait at the cabin until Stroud and Dolan returned with Fogal. Just then, McGinn drove up in his jeep. Behind him Richard Stoud braked with his dog, Apache.

Within seconds, Fogal drove up in his car, alone. He had received a call from the command post. Fogal started out for the Hollenbaugh cabin on his own and apparently passed

Stroud and Dolan en route. Fogal immediately identified the small dog as one of three belonging to the recluse.

The search dogs, now armed with the scent of the little dog, were straining at their leashes. They wanted to go west, toward the woods leading to Shade Mountain.

"We're going to take off. Radio in and tell them what we're going to do," Anderson told Plafcan.

However, rather than contact the men in charge at the command post, Plafcan gave the message to Sergeant William Kimmel, who said he would pass it on to Mitarnowski.

Plafcan, handling Weid, McGinn with King in tow and Richard Stoud, with Apache, made their way into the bottomland behind the Hollenbaugh cabin. Anderson followed with the two-way radio.

Fogal was directed to remain behind and advise Trooper Jack Stroud and Agent Dolan to follow when they arrived, at 9:45 A.M.

"The agent and the other officers decided to go ahead without you. They felt that the girl's life is in real danger now so they took off. You guys are supposed to follow," Fogal said.

"Shoot," Cox said into the telephone when he answered Peiffer's call. He glanced at the clock in the editorial department and noted it was 9:45 A.M.

After receiving directions, Cox replied, "I just wrapped up everything here and I'm getting ready to leave. See you in a little while," he said, and cradled the phone.

Cox swung by his home and picked up the sandwich Peiffer had asked for. He added a couple of cans of soft drink and told his wife he'd see her later that evening. He dropped only a hint that something big was going on right now in Shade Gap. "Keep the radio turned up today," he advised her.

McGinn had called a halt to the four-man posse as it was climbing a steep knob directly west of Hollenbaugh's cabin.

"We aren't tracking the little dog's scent anymore. Weid and King are now on the scent of Hollenbaugh and he can't be very far away," Mac said to Anderson.

"OK," Anderson replied. "We'll spread out and make our way to the top. Maybe we can spot him from there. Keep low to the ground and don't talk. We'll use hand signals from now on. And try not to make any noise." The other three nodded and began moving behind dogs whose neck hairs were stiff.

The men were tense as they crawled up the steep incline, fending off barbed bushes with their gun hands. The low growls of the dogs grew more menacing as they circled the knob and reached the summit. Mac was on the left with King, Anderson and Plafcan were with Weid, and Richard Stoud was with Apache.

"Mac, there's Hollenbaugh's little white dog," Anderson whispered, pointing through a clearing thirty feet away. It was watching the approaching group.

"Get down and release the dogs," Mac ordered, snapping King's leash. Plafcan and Stoud followed suit, and the three animals braced for the expected command to attack.

For several minutes, nothing happened. Weid then slowly made his way to Mac's side, where the trainer held him.

Anderson then motioned for Weid as he and Plafcan prepared to move toward the little white dog, which was frozen in its tracks. Weid slowly returned to Anderson's side. Mac and King inched their way to the right to circle behind the frightened animal. When he reached a point west of the dog, he motioned Anderson to move forward. Anderson released Weid and the large German shepherd slowly led the way, still waiting for the attack command.

It was then Mac saw the reflection of sunlight from a barrel of a shotgun sticking out of a bush. It was pointed directly at Anderson and Plafcan.

"Get down," Mac yelled, and gave the attack command to Weid. His eyes never left the gun barrel. Suddenly Hollen-baugh stood up from behind the bush.

Weid responded to the long awaited command and leaped, striking Hollenbaugh on the left side. The impact caused the gun to discharge into the air. The man and the dog disappeared.

A second later, another shot rang out and Weid rolled over a fallen tree and disappeared from sight.

Hollenbaugh rose immediately and cursed, "And I'll get you too, you son-of-a-bitch," pointing his rifle in the direction of Anderson.

The agent was bringing his pistol to a level position when the sniper fired again. Anderson spun and staggered out of sight.

Then Hollenbaugh turned to Mac, who had just given King the attack command. The rifle belched again but the bullet intended for Mac struck King in mid-air as he leapt toward his target. The animal yelped in pain and rolled over as it fell.

Mac dropped to the ground, pointed blindly in the direction of the sniper and got off three quick shots. Branches flew in every direction as the bullets whistled into the valley below.

Plafcan, still flat on his stomach in the opening, unloaded his revolver in the direction of the bush hiding the sniper. Again branches flew as the bullets were deflected by tree limbs and heavy underbrush.

Then silence. Only the unreal echoes of the gun reverberating in the valley below.

Let's move," Agent Dolan said to Trooper Stroud. But both froze in their tracks when they heard shooting. They exchanged worried glances.

"Christ Almighty. Let's go," Dolan yelled to Detective Broscius and Agent Dave Walker, who had just arrived at the cabin. "Watch the radio," Dolan commanded Fogal as the four, rifles and handguns ready, started west at a run.

Several minutes of silence followed before Mac rose from his prone position to look in the direction of the ambush. He could see nothing. Even the little white dog was gone. King, unconscious from his wound, twitched in the grass off to Mac's right. In the turmoil, Stoud was unable to get Apache to obey the attack command.

Plafcan rose to his knees after reloading his pistol, and aimed the weapon in the direction of the bush with both hands. He stood, openly raging, and walked woodenly toward the spot, finger tight on the trigger of his .38. He bent over the bush and cursed vehemently, "The bastard's gone."

Mac circled back to find Terry Anderson face down, blood spurting from his chest.

Plafcan ran to his side, took one look at his wounded friend and said, "Do what you can for Terry. I'll keep you covered." He stood upright over the two, daring another attack.

Stoud moved in and stood with his back to Plafcan, defending the opposite direction with his own gun.

When Mac cradled Anderson in his lap, attempting to stop the flow of blood from the chest wound, the agent opened his eyes for a second. "Mac," he said. Anderson mumbled something about the dogs, choked on his own blood and closed his eyes.

"He's dead," Mac cried. "Terry's dead! *Hollenbaugh, you bastard—you bastard! You're dead, Hollenbaugh! You're dead!*" Mac held Terry's limp body in his arms and sobbed.

"God damn. God damn," Plafcan cursed, looking at Terry. "Get help on the radio," he commanded with venom in his voice.

Mac cut the straps of the two-way radio from Terry's shoulders, and called for a doctor, an ambulance, a veterinarian and more police. "We've been attacked. Terry Anderson and the dogs have been hit. We need help fast," he called.

When the officer who answered asked for directions, Mac was unable to give a precise location—only west about three miles from Hollenbaugh's cabin.

Mac told the rescue party to follow the sound of their guns, they would fire rounds every two minutes to lead them. "And tell the guys who are coming to be careful," Mac cautioned.

"We're on our way. Sit tight," came the response.

Only after the conversation ended did Mac hear movement through the brush. It was one person, descending to the valley below.

Apache, who had not been given the scent of Hollenbaugh and therefore did not know whom to attack, walked over to the wounded King and licked his wound. Then twenty feet beyond the bush the Mountain Man had used as a shield, he found Weid, dead.

Peiffer's car made its way onto the dirt driveway leading to Hollenbaugh's cabin. Only minutes had passed since FBI agents and state police officers had taken off on foot toward the shots being fired on the knob. Four empty police vehicles, two with their motors running, stood as sentries as he stopped behind the last car in the row.

Fogal stood atop the rise. He didn't hear Peiffer drive up and was unaware of his presence until he was asked, "What's going on?"

"Don't ever do that!" Fogal yelled. When he regained his composure, he said, "There's been a shooting out there. At least one man was hurt from what I can gather, some dogs too. Who are you and what are you doing here?"

Peiffer identified himself and Fogal was relieved. The stiffness visibly went out of him. He was obviously glad for the company. "You can help me answer the radios in the cruisers if we get a call," Fogal said, turning his attention again west. "The officers just left to help. The others are apparently too hurt to move or are still under fire," Fogal said as the report of a rifle echoed across the valley. "Hear that?" he added.

"Yeah. My God. You think this is it? You think they got the kidnapper?" Peiffer asked.

"Sure hope so," Fogal said.

Just then a state police cruiser skidded into the driveway.

Trooper Kissner, accompanied by Trooper Fischer, leaped out of the car before it completely stopped, guns already in hand. They ran to the top of the hill and paused only long enough for Kissner to tell Peiffer that they were going across the valley to help out. Kissner held a rifle and Fischer an M-2 carbine. The expression on their faces left no doubt that they were ready for action.

"How about—" Peiffer started to ask.

"No. You stay here. Might even be wise if you two didn't present such good targets," Kissner added, indicating the upright stance Peiffer and Fogal had taken beyond the cabin.

The two civilians watched from stooped positions as the two officers, both in hunting garb, ran toward the shooting. Another state police cruiser and an unmarked car skidded to a stop near the cabin. Eight more men joined the dash west.

Yet another car appeared, blocking the driveway, preventing any more traffic from sealing in the vehicles already there. Four uniformed policemen stepped from the vehicle. One sporting corporal's stripes directed the other three to take positions along the road.

"No one gets in and no one gets out," he directed in a voice loud enough to carry to the top of the hill where Peiffer was still standing.

"Now ain't that a shame. No one gets in and no one gets out. That includes reporters and photographers." Peiffer grinned to himself. He was going to have a field day—if only his film lasted.

Kissner and Fischer reached a stream at the foot of the knob. There, they stopped to rest and think through their next move.

The pair had worked together for years. Each knew exactly what to expect from the other. They kept twenty feet of space between them, eliminating the possibility of being a single target.

Kissner signaled that they should stay below, following the stream south toward Burnt Cabins. They started moving south around the base of the knob, Kissner on the high side and Fischer east of the rapidly flowing stream. They had followed the stream only 200 yards when Kissner motioned for Fischer to come across the bank.

He leaped the brook and walked to where Kissner was kneeling, pointing at the mud. A freshly made footprint was visible, mud oozing back into the imprint. Another print was found several feet ahead.

"Whoever made the prints is just ahead," Kissner whispered. "He's running south." Their eyes traveled in that direction, searching out their quarry. But the heavy brush and trees blocked the view.

"Let's radio in what we have, and maybe they can stop him further south," Kissner said. He unstrapped the portable radio.

His report halted the immediate chase. "We have one officer killed. We don't want more. Stay put and we'll send help," came the reply over the radio.

A frustrated Kissner returned, "OK. But for Christ's sake, get someone down toward Burnt Cabins and along the Mountain Foot Road. He's headed that way and only minutes ahead of us."

While awaiting reinforcements, they discovered a different set of footprints in the same area, smaller and not as deep. They also found imprints of at least one dog, all headed south.

Within minutes, Lieutenant Roy Tittler and two other officers joined them and took stations which would protect the five from any attack.

Some distance north, the baying of dogs reached their ears as more law enforcement officers climbed the steep knob. But the immediate search for the sniper was over for the moment.

Detective Broscius and Agent Dave Walker were the first to arrive on the scene of the shooting. Broscius, armed with a rifle, added to the protection given the others while Walker gave his attention to Terry Anderson.

Within minutes, Jamieson arrived and took command of the situation. More agents and state police arrived at the scene, while a helicopter hovered overhead with a sharpshooter leaning out the window, scanning the area.

After speaking with Plafcan, Mac and Stoud, Jamieson ordered the trio to "Go get the bastard. We'll take over here. Pick up his trail and track him down." He ordered six other men to accompany them.

Apache, now certain of his quarry, picked up Hollenbaugh's trail and led the nine men, who were armed with long-range rifles, pistols and machine guns. The trail led almost directly to the foot of the summit and wound its way to the spot discovered earlier by Kissner and Fischer. Now, fourteen men and the dog started south, following the stream.

Less than a mile of travel, however, brought another halt to the posse. The dog had lost the trail in the stream. Every effort by Stoud to help Apache pick up the trail failed.

"I can't blame the dog," Mac consoled its handler. "He hasn't been working the trail. He just doesn't have the scent like Weid and King had," Mac said, fighting back tears.

When told Apache had lost the scent, Jamieson called off the search. Plafcan, Kissner, and Fischer were directed to Hollenbaugh's cabin. The rest of the posse was told to return to the scene of the shooting.

While he was making his way back to the top of the knob, Mac met John Strickler, the veterinarian who was hiking cross-country to give aid to King. The vet was accompanied by two men of the first aid squad from Orbisonia. They had heard or seen nothing in their cross-country trek.

The Mountain Man had vanished again—this time in brilliant sunlight, amidst dozens of armed men.

Cox decided that since the action was going to be closer to Burnt Cabins than Shade Gap, he'd head west on U.S. 30.

At 10:30 A.M., his bus was nearly upset by a gust of wind created by a state police cruiser pushing hard to Burnt Cabins.

Corporal Ray Hussack was at the wheel and Sergeant Jim Treas, officer in charge of the Chambersburg substation, sat in the front passenger's seat, waving Cox on.

He righted the wheel of the bus, jammed his foot to the floor and was hitting nearly seventy-five when it happened again. Another cruiser, this time with Corporal John Farrell at the wheel and FBI agent John Daane in the passenger's seat, passed at more than 100 miles an hour, rocking the bus on its wheels.

He knew that something was hot. "You just don't get the officer in charge of a barracks on the road that early in the day, traveling that fast for nothing," he thought.

"Gus, this is Milt. Get your ass in here, you're going to work," Trooper Milton Brown yelled into the telephone. He had been placed in command with the departure of Sergeant Treas, and was calling every off-duty member of the barracks.

Alexiou turned to his wife who had taken the day off from nursing duties at the Chambersburg Hospital to share his birthday. He grinned sheepishly and said, "Hon."

She just shook her head and pleaded, "No."

"'Fraid so. That was Milt. He said an FBI agent got it. Everybody goes," Gus lamented.

"It's okay. We'll celebrate this weekend. Get going and be careful. I want you back in one piece," she said. "Take the lunch with you. You may not get time to eat."

Gus, already dressed, nodded, kissed his wife and bolted to his car parked in the driveway of their suburban split-level home in Guilford Hills, east of Chambersburg.

Terry Seiple was sleeping when the telephone rang. He too, like Alexiou, had the day off—or so he thought. He rolled over in bed, lifted the telephone off its base and mumbled something unintelligible.

"Terry?" the caller asked.

"Yeah," the trooper said.

"This is Milt. Get in here right away. An FBI agent has

been shot over in Shade Gap and they're pulling the plug."

The calls were repeated over and over as Milt made contact with every officer on the roster. It didn't matter if the officer had just crawled into bed from night duty, or if he wasn't scheduled to come onto duty until that afternoon; he was called immediately into service.

Less than fifteen minutes after receiving the call, Seiple arrived at the barracks. Inside he met Ronnie Weigand, who, like himself, was supposed to have the day off.

Milt told them, "Ronnie, you and Seiple travel together. Go to the command post and get your assignment there. Don't plan on coming back home until this guy is tagged."

Seiple left the barracks armed with a machine gun. Ronnie, an expert marksman, took a rifle.

"Alexiou, you go with Bob Derwin, get your orders there and for Christ's sake, stay awake and keep your head on," Milt ordered. Alexiou picked out a rifle and Derwin a shotgun before running from the office.

The same scene was being repeated throughout the state.

Lieutenant Mitarnowski's request for additional troopers met with unparalleled response. Within minutes, an additional 250 state police were moving into the remote mountain area. When one barracks was emptied of officers, other officers were dispatched to fill the gap for normal police functions.

Agent Jamieson's call for additional men was expedited. Word was sent out through the eastern seaboard for 140 additional FBI agents. One of their ranks had been killed; he would be avenged quickly. Not often was an FBI agent killed in the line of duty. Anderson's death was only the sixth in the agency's history.

The Pennsylvania National Guard was activated, and men were called at work to respond. Trained dog handlers and their tracking dogs were called to Shade Gap from throughout Pennsylvania and other states.

Off-duty policemen were being called in from as far away as 150 miles. Sheriffs and their deputies, fire police and firemen, constables, Game and Fish Commission personnel, civilians with CB radios were asked to respond.

A massive army was converging on Shade Gap.

Cox sped under the Turnpike, jolted around a curve leading into Burnt Cabins and screeched to a stop inches from an officer who was boldly blocking the entrance into the village with his body.

"That's as far as you go, fella," the cop announced. "No one goes in or out," he added.

"I'm a reporter. Gotta get to the command post," Cox said.

"No way. Got orders to keep everyone out and that includes reporters," the cop replied.

"Who's in charge?" Cox asked, building up a head of steam. After covering the story for two years, he wasn't about to watch the climax from the outside.

"Far as you are concerned, I am," the cop sneered. "Shut that junk heap off and let it sit right there," he said, moving away to open a path for a police cruiser that had roared up, siren wailing.

Cox jumped down from the bus and started searching for a familiar policeman. He was nearly run over by Alexiou, who was behind the wheel of the cruiser.

"What the hell you doing here?" Alexiou yelled, stopping the cruiser short of Cox's legs. "Man, the action's up this way," Alexiou called out.

"Tell your comrade. He won't let me pass," Cox pleaded, pointing to the officer directing the traffic. "OK," Alexiou replied, moving the car ahead and stopping beside the traffic cop. Then he jammed the throttle and the car leaped ahead.

Cox didn't hear what Alexiou told the policeman, but the cop pointed the way and said, "OK, get out of here. If you want to get killed, that's your business."

Cox jumped into the bus, cranked over the engine and was moving ahead in seconds. However, another block stood in his way. On the northern perimeter of the village where Route 522 and Alternate Route 522 join, more policemen were blocking the road.

"You can't go up that way," an officer said. "No one allowed by this point unless he's a policeman."

"But I just got clearance to go from your teammate back there," Cox indicated the village.

"Sorry. Can't let you through this way," came the reply.

"How about using the alternate route?" Cox asked.

"Well . . ." the officer pondered.

"Thanks," Cox said, jamming the bus in gear and moving onto the narrow Mountain Foot Road leading to Neelyton. He was in motion before the officer regained his thoughts. He heard someone yell at him, and in the rearview mirror, saw the police waving him back. But he didn't stop.

Three miles north, he jerked the wheel left at Decorum. The road passed the spot where the kidnapping occurred.

Then it hit him. He had now gone at least four miles and had not passed one vehicle, had not seen one person. This area of the valley was deserted and it was still not noon. A chill passed over him and he pulled his pistol from its holster. He placed the loaded gun between his legs on the bucket seat and drove on, finally arriving at the construction of Route 522.

There he came upon more police than he had ever seen in one location at one time. He was within a couple of miles of the Hollenbaugh cabin now, and drove the rest of the way unchallenged.

The area around Hollenbaugh's cabin was jumping with action; dozens of police cars and civilian vehicles, including several pickup trucks with dog coops mounted in their beds, were spread out along the road and up the driveway. Cox stopped behind a pickup truck and grabbed his camera.

He searched the dozens of faces—grim and determined—and realized that he did not recognize a single person. They looked at him as though to compare his likeness to that of their quarry. Not one officer challenged his right to be there and apparently none cared. Then he saw Peiffer looking west over a mound of dirt.

"Where the hell ya been? How much film did you bring? Where's my breakfast?" Peiffer rattled, not waiting for answers in his excitement.

"Couldn't get through. Got a half-dozen rolls. In my coat pocket, in that order. Now, tell me what the hell goes on here?" Cox retorted, trying nonchalantly to hide his own excitement in order to calm his friend.

"Somebody was killed out there," Peiffer gestured toward the distant hills. "Don't know who yet but it won't be long now. Some cops took a jeep around the other way—the Mountain Foot dirt road—to bring the body back. They called for a vet so I guess some dogs were hurt too," he answered, calming down. "Man, I fell into this and came out smelling like a rose. You know, I'm the only photographer here and I've been burning film like it's going out of style. That's why I need more. You only brought a half-dozen rolls? That's not gonna be enough," he answered his own question.

"Let's get back to my car. I'll back the roll out of my camera and you can have it too, but give me what you've got because when I find out who was shot, I'm on the way back home. There's no way we're gonna get scooped today," Cox vowed.

During the five minutes Cox had been at the cabin, another half-dozen cars arrived, nearly blocking his bus. The new arrivals coalesced into tightly knit groups, gaining as much information as was available at the time from fellow officers who had arrived earlier. Their expressions were soon as grim as those of the men already there.

The exchange of film was made after Peiffer ate the sandwich Cox had brought for him. The two returned to the hilltop behind the cabin. They stopped beside Rocky Rockwell, who was torn with anguish. The knuckles on his right hand were white as he tried to choke the high-powered rifle he held.

"Damn, damn, damn," he repeated. "He was a good man.

One of the best agents I ever met. He's got a family too. Christ, this'll kill 'em. Damn," Rocky said again.

Cox and Peiffer, seeing this side of their friend for the first time, knew enough to keep silent. Cox reasoned that if Rocky kept talking, he would reveal who was killed, in his own way, in his own time.

"I remember when he took over the job in Harrisburg. Ten years ago it was. First impression I got was that he was a good man, a guy who knew what he was doing and knew the value of good relations with the 'staties.' I wasn't wrong either. We got to know him real well and he helped us as much as we helped him. My God, it just isn't fair. He wasn't even supposed to be up here; this wasn't his beat," Rocky volunteered.

The newsmen nodded silently, waiting while Rocky rambled on, still not revealing the identity of the victim. Cox swallowed back the question as Rocky spoke again.

"I just hope to hell someone gets to Anderson's wife and kids before some radio announcer blurts it out. How those guys find out the identities before the next of kin is notified is a wonder to me. At least you guys will have to wait until Terry's wife is notified," Rocky said.

Cox finally spoke, now that he was armed with what he needed to know. "Yeah. We won't be on the street until at least 2:30 this afternoon. She'll have been notified by that time." He watched Rocky to see if he had spoken out of turn. He hadn't. Rocky grinned slightly, relieved to hear someone else's voice beside his own.

"You know where Terry lived?" Cox asked.

"Yeah. In Camp Hill somewhere. He was forty-two, and a damn good man. You better say that in the article, because everybody liked him," Rocky demanded.

Peiffer interrupted. "Say, I think we might have a picture of Terry in the files. He was honored recently by the Exchange Club, as Policeman of the Year. I remember covering it and taking his picture along with Sergeant Snyder."

"Thanks," Cox responded, "I'm going to find a telephone and report in. You stay around here and keep the camera hot," he told Peiffer. "Rocky, take it easy. You'll get the guy soon. A gnat couldn't get out of the ring of cops around here unless you wanted him to," he said before leaving.

"I hope there ain't enough left of the bastard to scoop up when they meet up with him," Rocky answered.

Excitement of the newfound knowledge had Cox tensed up as he jockeyed his bus between the dozens of parked police and FBI vehicles at the end of the driveway. He headed toward Shade Gap and the nearest telephone but passed up a service station  grocery store midway to Shade Gap. It was filled with reporters who were waging a losing battle with police.

The public telephone at the service station at the intersection of Routes 522 and 641 was deserted. Everyone was trying to get where the action was, and Cox was grateful.

"Frank Young," Cox directed when the switchboard operator at the *Public Opinion* answered. She recognized his voice and started to pump questions, but he said, "Go back and lean over Frank's shoulder while I give it to him."

"You got the story?" Frank asked when he picked up the receiver.

"Yeah. The agent who was killed was Terry Anderson. We had a story and pix on him recently. Get someone on the files for background. In the meantime, figure out who you can send over here to pick up some of Ken's film. This guy Hollenbaugh is as good as dead now. These cops are in a dangerous mood and I don't want to leave here. They've probably got him trapped in the area north of Burnt Cabins. No way he can escape now."

Later that morning, Margie was busy painting the new apartment on State Street in Harrisburg, when a news bulletin interrupted the steady flow of music on the radio. It irritated her slightly.

"Wish they wouldn't do that," she said aloud to herself, stepping down from a ladder. She stretched, yawned and moved papers on the floor ahead of the ladder to catch the paint drippings. The noise drowned out the bulletin, but she caught a part of it. ". . . in addition, one dog was killed. Stay tuned for further details."

She snapped off the radio, wondering what was so important about a dog being killed.

Just then her friend Brenda arrived with a cold lunch. Margie was glad to rest for awhile.

"You really got a lot done," Brenda said, glancing around the apartment.

"When you're alone and have nothing better to do, work seems to get done quicker," Margie replied, unwrapping a sandwich.

"Oh, by the way. Someone from the FBI called and asked where they could get in touch with you. I told them. Whoever it was just thanked me and hung up," Brenda said. "You know what it's all about?"

Margie had a bite of sandwich in her mouth by the time Brenda had asked the question. She swallowed it and answered: "Don't know. But here comes Ron Brinkley and George Kean. I'm sure they'll know." Margie rose from the floor. She greeted the two agents who had become close friends over the years.

"Hi, Ron. Hi, George. What brings you guys here? You're not hunting for an apartment, I hope. This one isn't ready yet, " she said. Then she noticed the looks on their faces. Fear swept over her body.

"Margie . . . Terry's . . . been hurt," Ron stammered, reaching out for her. George took her other arm and both men steadied her as blood drained from her face. Her knees buckled as she looked from Ron to George.

"Is he . . .?" She didn't finish.

"Yes. My God, we're sorry," Ron stammered again. "What else can we say?" he asked pleadingly. She would have collapsed then had not both men been prepared. She sagged between them and began to cry.

Brenda put her arms around Margie and joined in her grief.

While Margie and Brenda sobbed, both agents remained silent. When the sobbing grew less intense, Ron said: "He didn't suffer. It was instant."

"I almost heard it on the radio just a little while ago," Margie said between sobs. "All I heard was that a dog was killed," she added.

Then, although she knew it was a false hope, she asked, "Are you sure it was Terry? Maybe there was a mistake?"

Ron answered her. "I wish to God I could say we weren't sure, but there's no mistake."

The sobs rose again and she needed support to stand.

In a little while, the four left the apartment, which was now a shattered dream of Terry and Margie Anderson—a place they had bought to add to the family income, a place which would make life a little easier in the years to come, a dream that Terry could no longer share.

Hundreds of cruisers began converging on the area from all points in the state. They came from as far west as Pittsburgh, and as far east as Philadelphia. By noon the already formidable complement of 200 state police had swelled to 500.

The additional 140 FBI agents summoned from Philadelphia, Washington, D.C., Pittsburgh and Baltimore began arriving.

Off-duty city, borough and township police, along with sheriffs' deputies, swarmed into the area. The Pennsylvania National Guard, alerted earlier in the morning, was completely activated and on the way.

Salvation Army mobile units from Philadelphia, Pittsburgh, Johnstown, Chambersburg, Tyrone, Huntingdon and Carlisle were rushed to Shade Gap to feed the growing crowds who were being spread out over a forty-mile perimeter.

Sixty-five portable electric generators were requisitioned for massive illumination; darkness was only a few hours away. Fire trucks by the dozens, from every company within a radius of 100 miles, responded with their lighting systems.

An emergency landing field was set up near Burnt Cabins for use by small reconnaissance planes and helicopters that kept a constant vigil during daylight hours.

Gasoline tank trucks, some loaded with aviation fuel and others with fuel to supply the land vehicles, whose motors would not be shut off during the night, were dispatched to the valley.

Letterkenny Army Depot in Chambersburg supplied hundreds of walkie-talkie radios for the lawmen assigned to the perimeter. Dozens of Army infrared searchlights were set up to probe the darkness where ordinary searchlights could not reach.

Civilian volunteers arrived by the hundreds. Massive traffic jams in the valley transformed the narrow roads into winding ribbons of steel. Motorists stopped along the Pennsylvania Turnpike near Fort Littleton to watch the spectacle unfold.

Spectators from Pennsylvania, New Jersey, Maryland, West Virginia, Virginia, Ohio, and Washington, D.C. watched in awe as official vehicles, emergency lights flashing, sped into the valley.

Troopers Alexiou, Derwin, Seiple and Weigand, along with FBI Agent Daane, were dispatched to secure and maintain an area west of Burnt Cabins where three summer homes were situated in the deep woods. They offered an ideal haven for Hollenbaugh and his captive. The men were told the murderer was headed in that general direction. They would be relieved when, and only when, Hollenbaugh was captured and Mary Lou was rescued.

Their assignment was described as a vital link in the forty-mile perimeter that was being set up to cordon off escape. They were the last ring of men to keep their quarry captive in the dense mountains.

The five left their cruisers blocking the dirt road to the cabins off Route 522. The vehicles were parked at the bottom of the hill where a wooden bridge crossed a stream.

Weigand, one of the best shots on the force, stayed close to the cars with a high-powered rifle, protecting the other four as they made their way slowly off the dirt road up the steep hill toward the cabins. Seiple carried a machine gun; Alexiou, Derwin and Daane, rifles, in addition to their handguns. The safeties were off the weapons, ready for action.

Despite the warmth of the spring sun, cold perspiration stood out on the men. The Mountain Man had already killed one agent and one dog and wounded another dog while under fire himself. The officers knew that he had nothing to lose by taking more lives.

They also knew that their quarry was a marksman without equal, a hunter who in all likelihood would settle as quickly as possible in the daylight hours, and wait in ambush. It left them nervous as they sprinted, then crawled, deeper into the woods.

Seiple and Daane chose to circle to the rear of the first building, while Alexiou and Derwin stormed the front. They had separated near the edge of the woods when they spotted a shed in the clearing, an open space that afforded no protection. They checked their watches and decided to wait fifteen minutes. This could give Seiple and Daane time to reach the rear and charge the building from the blind side.

"Suggestion," Alexiou offered Derwin. "You stay here and guard my flank. I'll rush the front of the place alone and if something happens, you put holes all through the sides of that shack," he said.

"Why you? I can do the rushing. I'm skinnier than you and I'd be less of a target," Bob Derwin replied.

"'Cause it's my idea, that's why me," Alexiou insisted. "Besides, with anything as skinny as you, people might think we didn't give the bastard a fair chance." He rose to a sprinting position. Checking his weapon, he made his move.

Derwin's finger tightened dangerously on the trigger of the rifle aimed at the old weathered building. *"Bon soir, mon ami,"* Alexiou said, and ran quickly across the forty feet of open space.

Seiple and Daane made the same decision: one would

storm the building while the other stayed behind. No sense in both getting their heads blown off at the same time. Seiple was elected to make the charge. He left the cover of woods at the same instant Alexiou was moving in front of him.

Alexiou burst through the lone door of the building, gun first. Seiple's machine gun was poking through the back window as Alexiou moved into view.

"It's me," Alexiou called out, his feet sending cinders ahead into the darkness. "OK," came the reply from Seiple.

Although it was near noon, clear and bright under the sun, the inside of the building was dark. Alexiou moved to one side of the doorway, his eyes following the sweep of the gun barrel in his hands.

Nothing. Lawn furniture, garden tools and a collection of junk greeted his eyes when they adjusted to the darkness. "Thank God," he said to himself.

They watched their next target from afar, a small farm house that had been remodeled into a summer place. It offered protection for anyone inside, and absolutely no protection for anyone outside.

Windows faced the shed in which the men hid. A screened-in porch surrounded the front of the house and an open porch gazed at them from the rear. A well and pump stood in bold relief on the front lawn, the only protection for anyone moving in from that direction.

"Let's charge right up to the side of the house, stay under the windows and then separate to the front and back," Alexiou offered, wiping the nervous sweat from his forehead.

"Sounds good," Seiple replied. He stepped to the doorway and waved Daane first, then Derwin, to move them into a better position to cover the action.

"Had the strongest urge to yell like a banshee when I was running over here," Alexiou offered.

"So did I. Thought I would feel better if I could holler like hell," Seiple replied, shifting the machine gun nervously as he waited, watching Derwin move into position.

"Race you to the house," Alexiou said, when Derwin gave the go-ahead signal. Both men took off, running in crouched positions. They bumped into the side of the building simultaneously.

Since Gus was on the left he moved in the direction of the screened-in porch while Seiple approached the rear. As each passed under a window they checked them and found they were locked from the inside.

With his gun in front of him, Seiple jumped onto the back porch and stood to the side of the wooden door. He reached across with his left hand to try the knob, and found it unyielding. He held the gun to the right, and yanked hard on the door. It was bolted from the inside.

He jumped down from the porch and circled the building, trying each window in turn. He found none open. Alexiou, his gun leading the way, stooped low along the screened-in porch and made his way to the front screen door. A quick look revealed it was hooked from inside. He pushed the gun barrel into the screen, separating it from the door frame far enough to allow him to reach in and unlatch the door, just as Seiple appeared from the far side of the house.

Alexiou motioned him to follow, and both moved onto the screened-in porch, training a gun on each of the two front windows.

Alexiou then reached for the front door knob. It turned easily under the pressure. The door fell ajar. Alexiou kicked the door wide open.

They burst into the living room of the house and again were greeted with a darkened interior. Not, however, quite as dark as the shed. Sunlight through shades and curtains afforded some light. The building was fully furnished but unoccupied.

They had secured their second building, and were ready now for the third, a building deeper in the woods and, from this point, out of sight. When Alexiou and Seiple stepped outside of the cabin they motioned for Daane and Derwin to join them, and for Ronnie Weigand to move one cruiser in closer.

After he moved the car to a spot near the clearing, Ronnie sought a better vantage point to protect his fellow officers. He forded a creek, crept through a marshland, and stopped adjacent to a farm pond. From there he could see the roof of the third building.

The four men now moved in the woods again to approach the next building. They stayed clear of the dirt road. Then, about 50 yards from the place, all four men dropped to their stomachs. They had heard voices in the distance.

Seiple, who had been leading the group, rose and stepped to a clearing. "Well, look," he said to the other three.

They saw three men, a woman and two kids blissfully cleaning and repairing the building, totally unaware of what was going on around them. The four lawmen laughed nervously before Alexiou stepped into the clearing and called out for the man closest to them to come over.

He hesitated when he saw three troopers, their uniforms covered with mud and leaves, and a fourth man in hunting attire, all carrying weapons. His eyes were glued on Seiple's machine gun.

"Who are you and what the hell are you doing here?" Alexiou asked.

"I'm the owner. I'm an attorney from Washington, D.C. We're here cleaning the place up for the weekend," the man answered.

"Don't you know what's going on here?" Alexiou asked. "Man, you gave us a fright." They poured out the story to the attorney who hadn't bothered to listen to the radio or read a newspaper for more than a week.

Within minutes, the owner rounded up his family and two carpenters and was driving down the lane to safety. Before he left, however, he turned the keys to the cabin over to the men. He told them they were welcome to the food he had brought for the weekend. The four then searched the cabin from top to bottom, in the event Hollenbaugh had been hiding, waiting for the right time to make his break or to hold the family as hostages. They found nothing.

As they prepared to make a search of the last building in

the area, they were joined by a sheriff from Perry County and two deputies. All were armed with shotguns.

The seven men moved to the last building, a two-and-a-half-story structure that had seen better days. It had been a farmhouse at one time and was now converted into a summer place.

The group surrounded the building and approached from all sides. It was unlocked and the seven divided the task of searching from the cellar to the attic. They found no indication that anyone had been in the building since last fall. Dust and cobwebs covered the furniture and doorways.

Only then did the men feel some relief from the tension.

Sergeant Jim Treas and Corporal Ray Hussack had been stationed along the Mountain Foot Road for less than two hours when the mobile canteen arrived. After serving the men sandwiches, hot drinks and fruit, the unit moved down the road, passing out of sight around a curve south of the Hollenbaugh cabin.

It was followed shortly by a State Department of Highways truck. The truck stopped beside the two cruisers, filled the tanks and then moved onto the next stop.

The operation was working like a well-tuned machine. Orders followed, directing the men on the perimeter to be doubly alert. "You men will have to keep watch on both sides of the road. Trooper Bidelspach has identified Hollenbaugh and Mary Lou Broderick visually. He saw them cross the Mountain Foot Road some time ago, heading toward Burnt Cabins," the radios blared out.

The sighting was verified with photographs shown the trooper at the command post. It was made near the spot where Treas and Hussack were now stationed.

Officers from the command post were dispatched along the entire route of guards to warn them individually and direct them to be careful. The victim was still alive, seven days after the kidnapping.

The news was immediately sent to the Broderick home,

where smiles appeared on the faces of the family for the first time in a week.

Other vehicles made their way along the perimeter, distributing equipment to sustain the long watch. Portable spotlights were handed out to each cruiser, to supplement the vehicle's lights. The men were told that the lights were not to be turned off for any reason during the night. Walkie-talkies, provided by the Army, were given to nearly every officer. Cigarettes, pipe tobacco and cigars were handed out to the men around the forty-mile perimeter.

Corporal Grant Mixell and Trooper Richard Bodine of Carlisle arrived at the command post shortly before noon. They were given a map and assigned to guard the farm home of Luther Rubeck, along Route 522, midway between Burnt Cabins and the Fort Littleton Interchange of the Pennsylvania Turnpike. The turnpike passed several hundred feet south of the farm, offering an escape route for the Mountain Man if he made it through the perimeter.

Lieutenant James D. Barger of Greensburg was in charge of the thirty-one-man detail spread along the west section of the perimeter. He stationed the two Carlisle officers at the gate across a dirt driveway leading north into the mountains. The gate was directly across the road from the Rubeck home. A small wooden bridge spanned a creek near the gate.

"From the direction the man and girl were traveling, we stand a good chance of being the last hurdle in their way," Barger told Mixell and Bodine. "Make sure you check everyone coming through here, and don't leave your post until you clear it with me," he said before moving on to give orders to the rest of the men under his command.

The afternoon sun pushed the temperatures into the low 80's. Mixell decided the reflection of sunlight from something deep in the woods should be checked out. Lieutenant Barger, who had returned earlier, agreed; and he accompanied Mixell on the reconnaissance mission, leaving Bodine and another office to guard the driveway.

A master key unlocked the gate, and Bodine closed it behind the cruiser as it crossed the bridge. They stopped again at a second gate on the other side of the bridge. The same procedure was followed. They had traveled a quarter of a mile when they saw a hunting cabin. A garage and an outbuilding complemented the cabin. Mixell readied a rifle while Lieutenant Barger unholstered his handgun. They approached the building on foot.

Peering through windows, the men found the outbuilding empty. A small farm tractor and a car filled the garage. The doors and windows of the garage were secured from the outside; entry was unnecessary. A toilet attached to the side of the garage was also locked from the outside.

Mixell received permission from the command post to force the lock on the front door of the cabin.

Inside, they found a well-stocked cabin, but it had not been used recently. Dust and cobwebs were undisturbed.

However, in searching the dwelling, two rifles and a shotgun were discovered, along with enough ammunition to fill a waste basket. They returned to the highway, where the guns and ammunition were locked in the trunk of Mixell's cruiser. An inventory was made and turned over to the officer in charge.

Mixell told Bodine to keep watch while he walked down the road to the Rubeck farm and called the owner of the cabin. He informed him the guns and ammunition had been confiscated.

The first contingent of the Pennsylvania National Guard arrived at Shade Gap early in the afternoon, five trucks and two personnel carriers under the command of Captain Robert Appleby. Twenty in the group were assigned to set up a base near Burnt Cabins.

The alert later brought in even more men and equipment, including jeeps and half-tracks, from Troop K, 104th Armored Cavalry Regiment, Chambersburg; and Troop G, 2nd Squadron, 104th Armored Cavalry Regiment, Waynesboro. There were now 260 uniformed soldiers on hand armed with everything under a bazooka. The soldiers from

Chambersburg and Waynesboro, however, were not given ammunition. A policy of the Guard is that the men and the bullets are separated en route to an assignment. The men arrived promptly, but the ammunition truck was delayed.

The police departments in Johnstown and Pittsburgh, the Fairmount Park guards of Philadelphia, and the Pennsylvania Electric Company dispatched twenty-two police dogs and handlers to Shade Gap. More dogs from the K-9 Academy were flown from Arkansas, arriving late in the day. However, they were airsick and unable to track. Most were assigned to the perimeter duty.

To make sure immediate attention would be available for the dogs, Captain Blessing and Sergeant Ronkle, base veterinarian team, Air Force, Harrisburg, were summoned and placed on stand-by in the event they were needed at the command post.

The nearest hospital, the Fulton County Medical Center, McConnellsburg, was ordered on alert in case men were wounded. The Chambersburg Hospital, thirty-five miles away, was also warned.

The U.S. Naval Air Station in Willow Grove dispatched three helicopters to Shade Gap, using the baseball field at the picnic grounds for landing and refueling. The helicopters were to be used in reconnaissance missions over the deep woods.

A building contractor, commissioned to construct a tunnel under the Tuscarora Mountains for the Turnpike, installed lighting for the helicopters for night landing.

By mid-afternoon, more than 1000 men—law enforcement officers, sailors, civilians, constables, deputy sheriffs, firemen, even the entire forces of the Pennsylvania Fish Commission from the Franklin and Honesdale districts, and the Game Commission from as far away as Bethlehem and the South Central District Office—were on hand, forming a human chain around the forty-mile perimeter.

Little attention was paid to anyone attempting to get inside the perimeter. The more volunteers, the better.

Anyone attempting to get out, however, was subjected to

a search, and his vehicle screened by lawmen blocking all exits.

Burnt Cabins, the tiny northern Fulton County hamlet, was turned into a national newsroom, as reporters and photographers from newspapers, magazines, radio and television swarmed in to cover the story. They arrived by car, truck, jeep, bus and plane from New York, Washington, D.C., Baltimore, Philadelphia, Pittsburgh, central Pennsylvania, Maryland and West Virginia.

After police, unable to cope with the crowds, closed the road north to all traffic, the reporters gathered in the triangular area in the center of the village. They pressed the dining facilities to their peak, until parishioners of two village churches came with sandwiches, cookies and hot coffee.

Correspondents had to wait in a long line to use the one available pay telephone outside a taproom. Others leaned against buildings and cars waiting for some news.

They looked to the north, where helicopters and small planes swooped low over the mountain peaks where the Mountain Man was supposedly cornered.

Countless police and FBI vehicles passed the roadblock. Occasionally a car carrying a dog would drive through the roadblock.

To the rear of the triangle, where the Turnpike was visible, cars and tractor trailers were parked along the dual highway, their occupants staring intently toward the mountains. Most used binoculars, but a few had powerful telescopes.

Workers on their way home and schoolchildren who lived along the blocked road were stranded for hours. They sat in their cars and buses, and were interviewed by bored reporters who decided to add local color to their stories.

The lives of the local residents were disrupted. At nearly every house, porch steps were occupied by strangers. Mothers tried vainly to keep the children inside, but it was a unique experience, not to be missed behind closed doors. A circus-like atmosphere reigned, just two miles from where a murderer earlier in the day took the life of Agent Terry Anderson.

Finally, at dusk, press representatives were allowed into the blockaded area. The long wait in Burnt Cabins was over, and the highway to Shade Gap and the command post was a speedway of newsmen's cars.

Joe Jamieson, FBI agent in charge, read the warrant issued for William D. Hollenbaugh, wanted for the murder of Agent Anderson.

The news was flashed to the world. Photographers, now armed with something substantial on film, raced from the area to Harrisburg, where processing and printing establishments were working overtime to accommodate the press.

No mobilization for war was handled with more swiftness or singleness of thought than the war against the Mountain Man. Odds on his winning were already reduced to 1 in 2,000.

Cox easily made his way back to the valley after delivering film for the day's edition and parked his VW bus a half-mile from the Hollenbaugh cabin. A base camp had been set up at the bottomland near the cabin. The command post was still the base of most operations, but Agent Jamieson and Lieutenant Mitarnowski were now at the front line, passing orders via messenger vehicles since no telephone could be installed immediately. No substantial directive passed over the radio waves of the police cruisers.

Walking past the long lines of vehicles, Cox was amazed at the number of FBI agents along the road who stripped, shedding street clothing for attire more suited to the locale and occasion. Under every agent's jacket was a bullet-proof vest.

They left their cars in hunting garb, with knee-high boots, caps, jackets and knives. But they stood out in the crowds: most of them toted tommy guns—not the normal weapons for hunters.

Cox found Peiffer atop the knoll behind the Hollenbaugh cabin, two cameras strapped around his neck, a cup of coffee in one hand, a half-eaten sandwich in the other. He noticed that the Salvation Army had moved one of its mobile units onto the embankment beside the cabin, supplying food and drink to all takers.

"Hold my sandwich. I gotta reload the camera. They're bringing in Anderson's body soon, and the body of the dog. And I'm almost out of film," Peiffer said. "Don't eat it," he added. Then he saw an ambulance moving up the driveway to the cabin.

"They're getting ready. We can position ourselves awhile and get prepared for some shots," Cox suggested, but Peiffer was already reading the sun and the angles for the best pictures. The two moved closer to the cabin with the sun against their backs.

"I'll stay here on the bank with the telephoto lens. You can get closer down there," Peiffer suggested when they saw the jeep, carrying Anderson's body on a stretcher over the back seat.

"They had to go back with the jeep. They couldn't carry the body out of the steep hills. There's a logging road that leads right up to where the shooting took place," Peiffer answered the unasked question.

Four agents escorted the body. They hung onto the sides of the jeep for more than eight miles from the scene of the murder—just a mile and a half across the hills to the west.

In minutes agents transferred Anderson's body from the jeep into the ambulance, handling the lifeless form gently. Two carloads of agents and state police escorted the ambulance as it made the fifty-mile drive to a hospital in Harrisburg where Margie and her children were waiting.

Soon, another jeep approached, and the scene was repeated again as McGinn's dog, Weid, was brought in from the deep woods. Mac sat by the dog on the rear seat. He was covered with the blood of the agent as well as that of his two dogs. Tears streamed down his face when Weid's body was loaded into a veterinarian's car to be taken for disposal. King had been rushed to Chambersburg in another car and had already undergone surgery.

Dr. Strickler, at the Chambersburg Animal Hospital, operated on King for nearly four hours. By late afternoon, word was received at the command post that McGinn's dog would survive and, after long recuperation, would probably be able to track again.

Pellets from the shotgun blast entered the dog's shoulder, shattering its left front leg, passed through its body, and exited from the lower part of its neck. The dog had lost large amounts of blood. McGinn was told that King would be released the next day to the University of Pennsylvania for better care of his leg. Tears of grief and rage sparkled in McGinn's eyes. He silently hoped he would be there when Hollenbaugh was captured, or killed.

Later in the evening, Grant Mixell stopped a car which approached the locked gate leading to the A. C. Shonek cabin off Route 522, which he and Barger had searched earlier in the day. The driver identified himself as Francis Sharpe of Conemaugh. He flashed a deputy sheriff's card, and said he was a friend of the owner and was going to spend the night in the cabin.

"That's not smart. There's a lunatic somewhere in the woods. He's already killed one man and has nothing to lose by taking another life," Mixell warned Sharpe.

"I can take care of myself," Sharpe said, opening the trunk of his Rambler and proudly showing a loaded 30.06 rifle.

"That thing won't do you any good back there tonight," Dick Bodine warned Sharpe.

"OK, but I'm still going to spend the night in a bed in that cabin. No one in his right mind would approach this area with as many guys on guard as you have here," Sharpe said.

"Hollenbaugh isn't in his right mind," Bodine answered.

"I'm going back there and go to bed," Sharpe said defiantly.

"OK, but if you run into trouble, fire a couple of shots into the air," Mixell said unlocking the gate to the dirt driveway.

"I'm hungry," Mixell announced a short time later. "It's after 8:30 and we haven't eaten. Flip you to see who goes into Burnt Cabins for something," he said. Bodine stayed behind and Mixell drove to the little community.

The grocery store was doing a booming business despite the hour, with lawmen and civilians taking advantage of the fresh food, meat and drinks.

Mixell picked up lunch meat, milk and bread. Then after he asked for cigarettes, he asked, "How much do I owe you?"

"Nothing. The least I can do for you is give you something to eat. Now don't make me mad. Just pick up the stuff and get out of here. And good luck. I hope you get him soon," was the merchant's response.

As he drove back, Mixell marveled at these people and shared the suffering they had undergone for the past two years.

"We'll get him," he promised himself.

Alexiou and Derwin, still on duty at 7:30 P.M., took positions at the edge of the clearing near the cabins west of Burnt Cabins and settled down to an expected quiet night of surveillance. Both were pleased to see that the group had grown in size now to more than a dozen men, including FBI agents, state police and deputy sheriffs. At least now they were not alone.

Darkness was falling rapidly in the area. The last car was hidden from sight and the men were positioned within sight of each other. The shadows deepened when Daane made his way to each man, cautioning him to be as quiet as possible, and to keep alert.

Alexiou and Derwin had been gone a half-hour, and had just returned when Seiple first heard the little dog barking as it ran toward them from the logging road. Everyone in the detail knew Hollenbaugh still had two dogs with him and this one perfectly fit the description of one of the animals. Seiple sank deeper into the six-inch-tall grass, his weapon pointed beyond the dog.

It had come into the clearing not 15 feet from the road and about 100 feet south of the second cabin, behind which a steep incline led directly into the mountains.

The dog bounded into the center of the clearing, yapping

at the hidden men. For five minutes, the men stared silently at the dog and the deep woods behind it, checking for any possible movement. Nothing moved in the dead calm.

Daane then whispered to Alexiou, Seiple and Weigand. "Circle around the dog. We've got to get him. The rest of you keep your eyes back there near the dirt road. Blow hell out of the first thing that moves."

The four men approached the dog in the center of the clearing, coaxing it to come to them. The dog walked to Alexiou. He picked it up. They moved back again into the shadows, where Alexiou removed his tie and fashioned a collar and leash for the dog.

Derwin offered him a piece of cake from the food that Alexiou had brought earlier. The dog ate greedily. Then they tied the necktie to a tree and waited a half-hour while the dog barked, hoping to lure Hollenbaugh out of hiding.

"I'll call the command post and report this. You guys stay under cover until I get back," Daane said, when he realized the ruse hadn't worked.

In a short time he returned with orders for Alexiou and Seiple to take the dog in one of the cruisers and return to the Hollenbaugh cabin, where Jamieson and Mitarnowski would be waiting.

"The rest of us will stay here and keep watch," Daane ordered.

When they arrived at the cabin, residents of the area who knew Hollenbaugh recognized the little white dog. Hollenbaugh's other dog, found early that morning, made the identification positive with its welcoming bark.

Cox met Alexiou and Seiple when they arrived, and stuck close. His friendship with the policemen paid off. They gave him the complete story and the knowledge of where the hunt was now being concentrated, and the most likely place where Hollenbaugh would be headed.

The area around the cabins was to be sealed off and Alexiou was directed to lead a caravan of men back to reinforce the men still on watch. Seiple was directed to keep the dog with him for the rest of the night and, in the morning, return to the cabins and turn the dogs loose, with a small army of tracking dogs and peace officers at his side.

This was to be the final push, with the hunted man's dogs leading the posse directly to him, wherever he was hidden in the mountains.

# THE EIGHTH DAY    *Wednesday, May 18, 1966*

Hundreds of cars, trucks and Army vehicles, none more than seventy-five feet apart, formed a solid line of light, all pointing in the same direction, around the four-mile perimeter from Burnt Cabins to the Mountain Foot Road south of Shade Gap. It was 2 A.M.

Nowhere along the perimeter was the light shield broken. One could see anything or anyone without difficulty. The light provided perfect surveillance of every officer along the perimeter. When one space between vehicles did not have light enough to read a newspaper, another car was moved into the gap to increase the brightness.

Shortly after 3 A.M., copies of Hollenbaugh's picture were distributed to every man in the perimeter.

Many were disappointed at the likeness that stared directly out of the photo. He looked nothing like a man who could have created the terror this valley had lived under for two years. Yet here was the man, expressionless for the camera, who had shot down an FBI agent, killed a dog and wounded another while under fire from expert marksmen.

Here was the man who had kidnapped a seventeen-year-old girl and had made fools out of hundreds of police, taunting them with his elusive presence.

Here was the man who reportedly had blown the leg off one man, shot the gun out of the hands of a woman, crippling her, fired volleys into a moving vehicle, hitting a bottle in the mouth of an infant, attacked two other women, and during it all, lived in the midst of the residents of the valley, undetected.

Here was the man who was described as over six feet tall, thin, fat, stocky, never under five feet nine inches. Here was the Mountain Man, the sniper, the Phantom of the Valley, Bicycle Pete, who didn't own a car, who couldn't drive and had no known friends who could have lent him one, but left automobile tire tracks behind at scenes of earlier crimes. Here was the man whose sunken cheeks belied the description given by every one of the former victims and the Broderick children, who had said he was full-faced.

Mac McGinn, who less than twenty hours before had been face to face with the man who shot and killed Anderson and his dog, Weid, said upon viewing the photo, "This man bears little resemblance to the man I saw shoot Anderson."

But now, the army of men knew their enemy on sight.

At 6 A.M., Cox and Peiffer were stopped by police and National Guardsmen at Burnt Cabins. No amount of pleading, coercion or attempted bribery budged the men at the roadblock. They said no one could go inside the perimeter before daylight.

"Nothing's going on up there now but men sleeping. You stay put till daylight, then we'll let you through and not before," an officer said, closing the discussion. The newsmen left for coffee at the hotel, resigned to the delay.

At 6 A.M., Terry Seiple was directed to join a party of more than forty state police and FBI agents, along with McGinn, who had a new dog, and several other handlers and their dogs. Seiple was directed to carry the little white dog on what was to be a final push into the woods.

The ten-car convoy moved down Route 522 and turned

into the dirt lane that led to the three cabins that Alexiou, Daane, Derwin and others had kept under surveillance throughout the night. It was from this point that the final drive was to begin.

At 6 A.M., an Army truck dropped off three more Franklin County National Guardsmen at the Rubeck farm along Route 522.

Grant Mixell met the three Guardsmen and suppressed a curse when they informed him they had no ammunition for their brand new M-1 rifles. He stationed one Guardsman north of the Rubeck barn, one south of the house and the other south of his patrol car. "OK. Your guns aren't loaded, so don't get brave. If the killer shows up, everyone take cover and stay there until I tell you to come out."

There were no heroes in the group; they all promised to bury themselves if the occasion demanded.

Mixell informed them that dozens of men would be heading this way from the mountains in an attempt to flush Hollenbaugh out of hiding.

Just then Rubeck and his two sons crossed the road toward the barn.

"You think it will be safe to go to work today?" Rubeck asked Mixell.

"I'm sure it will be OK. We have enough men here to protect your family if it becomes necessary," Mixell assured him.

"I'll be leaving in a half-hour or so," Rubeck replied.

It was 6:30 A.M. when McGinn passed clothing to all the dog handlers, who in turn pressed the articles against the noses of their dogs to prime them with the scent of their quarry. The clothes had been taken from Hollenbaugh's cabin and Mary's home. Although they hadn't been worn for at least a week, the dogs reacted immediately.

The scents of the hunted man and the girl were picked up a few feet from where Seiple had been stationed before the little dog came into the clearing—so close that the man and girl could have reached out and touched Seiple while he watched the clearing the night before.

"OK. We've got the scent. The dogs are ready to track.

Let's move out," McGinn directed, holding his dog tightly as it strained to take up the chase. The 40-man hunting party started out across the clearing toward the south, in the general direction of Burnt Cabins.

Seiple, carrying the white dog, protected his chest with the animal. "Maybe if Hollenbaugh sees the little dog, he won't shoot at me," Seiple reasoned. They moved out of sight of the twenty men who were told to remain behind, in case Hollenbaugh backtracked.

At 6 A.M., Deputy Sheriff Francis Sharpe arose from the bed in the Shonek cabin and stretched. He felt rested and relaxed after a good night's sleep.

Still dressed in pajamas, he headed for the bathroom before dressing and joining the men at the end of the lane. The bathroom and shower had to be entered from outside the cabin. He opened the cabin door and squinted into the rising sun. He thought to himself it was going to be a good day, shivered at the sudden chill of the morning, and made his way to the other door. He switched on the light. Nothing happened, and he thought the light had burned out. Still, there was some light entering the bath from its lone window, and he sat down on the commode.

To his left the shower curtains moved slightly, and Sharpe rose to his feet.

"Don't run or I'll shoot you," a voice commanded from behind the curtain. But Sharpe already had momentum and took a step toward the doorway.

A shot rang out, deafening in the little room, and Sharpe felt a pain in his stomach. He grabbed his middle and watched warm blood ooze between his fingers.

Then he turned toward the shower and saw a man step out, holding a .32 caliber pistol in his right hand. A young girl stepped out behind him.

"See, I told you not to run. You're going to get me out of here," the gunman said, matter of factly. He might as well have been speaking about the weather; there was no inflection in his voice.

"My God, you shot me. I've got to get to a doctor. I've got to get to the hospital," Sharpe said.

"The only thing you're going to do is drive me and Mary out of here. Now get the hell into the cabin and get some clothes on or I'll kill you."

"OK. OK. I'll drive you out of here, but I've got to get to a doctor or I'll die," Sharpe pleaded, gripping the bleeding wound with both hands.

"Shut up and get going," the man said again, this time pushing Sharpe in the small of the back with the barrel of the gun.

Sharpe moved out of the bathroom with the man and girl trailing. She had not spoken.

"Get the hell dressed, and do it quick," the man said.

"You're Hollenbaugh and you're the girl, aren't you?" Sharpe asked as he walked toward the bedroom.

"Get those damn clothes off and get dressed, or you're a dead man," Hollenbaugh shouted, showing the first sign of nervousness. He glanced around the room and then asked, "Where's the guns?"

Sharpe didn't answer, but asked the girl instead, "How bad is the wound? Do you think I'm gonna die?"

She didn't answer, just stood outside the doorway behind Hollenbaugh, watching the men.

Sharpe removed his blood-soaked pajamas, dropped them onto the floor and pulled on his trousers and a shirt. He stuffed his sockless feet into shoes and rose from the bed where he had been sitting. All the while, Hollenbaugh had been talking to Mary Lou, but Sharpe, his mind reeling with pain, could not catch the conversation.

"All right, let's get the hell out of here. You drive. We'll get in the back. If you try to signal anyone, I'll blow your goddamn head off." Hollenbaugh and the girl settled into the rear seat of Sharpe's green Rambler.

"There are two gates out at the end of the road. I'll have to get out and open them," Sharpe said.

Hollenbaugh didn't answer.

"Can I drive to a doctor right away? I think I'm bleeding to death," Sharpe pleaded.

"You get us out of here and I don't give a damn where you go or what you do. Now drive, or I'll kill you, I swear," Hollenbaugh said.

Then he raised a shotgun off the floor and rested the barrel on the back of the driver's seat.

Sharpe started the motor and slipped the car in gear, heading down the dirt road to where he knew the troopers waited.

The pain nearly caused him to black out and the car veered off the road. The bump against the drainage ditch snapped him back to consciousness, and he swerved back onto the dirt road.

"You son-of-a-bitch. You do that again and it'll be the last thing you ever do," Hollenbaugh warned from the back seat.

Sharpe glanced into the rearview mirror and saw the reflection of the girl seated beside Hollenbaugh. Then he saw Hollenbaugh's left hand reach for her head and push.

"You get down on the floor and stay there. We don't want any goddamn cop to see a girl," he spat out as the car rounded the curve on the dirt road. The highway came into view.

Sharpe could see a police cruiser close to the second gate parked on the north side of the highway. He also saw two officers and a number of soldiers standing guard.

Mixell looked up as the car came into view. "Here comes Sharpe's car. Guess he made it through the night with no problems. Boy, I sure would have loved spending the last hours in bed," he said to Bodine, pointing to the green Rambler making its way slowly down the dusty road.

"Yeah. I could use a nice soft sack myself about now. Wonder how long it'll be before we're relieved?" Bodine asked as both men walked from the cruiser toward the gate. Even though the officers recognized the car, it was normal procedure to check it out.

Mixell shrugged. "Don't know. We may have to spend the

rest of the day here unless they get Hollenbaugh. Lord knows where they'll come up with this many men as replacements."

"You try to signal them and the first bullet goes into the back of your head," Hollenbaugh warned from the back seat.

"Please don't shoot me again. I won't try to signal. But I've got to get out and open the gates," Sharpe reminded him.

"OK. But remember, I've got you in my sights," Hollenbaugh warned as the car braked to a stop at the first gate.

Sharpe got out of the car, opened the first gate, then got back behind the wheel. He drove the car to the other end of the wooden bridge, stopped and got out again to open the second gate.

As the officers reached a point midway between the cruiser and the lane, Mixell stopped short. His hand reached out and touched Bodine. "I think I see someone in the back seat of Sharpe's car."

"My God . . . that looks like the guy," Bodine replied as both men snapped open their holsters.

Sharpe reached to open the second gate when he suddenly called out to the officers, "My God. I'm shot. I need help. They made me bring them down," he yelled at the approaching officers with one hand on the closed gate and the other clutching his stomach.

Mixell saw then that Sharpe's shirt was covered with blood.

"Take cover," Mixell called out, dropping to one knee and lifting his handgun out at the same time. His eyes turned back to the car. He saw a shotgun poke out of the side window, aimed over the right front fender.

"It's Hollenbaugh. Hit the deck," Mixell yelled as both men dropped. They no sooner landed on their stomachs than the first shot rang out, the slug ricochetting off the hard roadbed. Stones stung the faces of the two men.

Bodine started to roll toward the opposite side of the road when he drew Hollenbaugh's fire. Another shot boomed across the valley, and again stones kicked up, this time between the men as Bodine rolled away.

Mixell pointed his service revolver at the car and got off two quick shots before he rolled in the same direction as Bodine, toward the drainage ditch along the south side of the road.

Mixell called out to Bodine, "We can't get out of the line of fire this way. Let's run." He didn't hear a reply, but as he rose to a crouch, he saw Bodine do the same.

They ran in a zigzag , and dived head first into another ditch as more shots spat at their feet, stones flying in every direction. Bullets zinged over their heads, whining into the distance toward the turnpike.

"Christ, there must be more than one guy shooting," Mixell gasped, sucking air into his lungs.

"Or the son-of-a-bitch has an automatic," Bodine replied. "My God, what a shot," he added in admiration of Hollen- baugh, who had suddenly become his mortal enemy.

"You all right? You hit?" Mixell asked, suddenly con- cerned at the tone of Bodine's voice. He glanced quickly at him and found him doubled in pain.

"I don't know. I don't feel right," Bodine answered. Just then, several more shots whined over them, stones and dirt falling into the ditch on their heads. The slugs hit the soft shoulder of the road, directly over the spot where they lay.

"You got any cover? Can you get a shot off?" Mixell yelled above the noise of the booming sound reverberating in the field behind them.

"No. The bastard has me pinned down. I can't get up to see where to aim," Bodine shouted back.

Mixell said, "OK. Stay put. I'm going to see if I can reach that pole and use it for a shield."

He crawled along the ditch for a short distance, then raised his head and shoulders behind the protection. Slowly, he raised his gun along the side of the pole to chest level, then just as slowly peered around it. He could see the car.

Pointing, not aiming, Mixell squeezed off a shot and saw that it hit the right rear door.

The return fire caused Hollenbaugh to panic. He jerked open the left rear door and leaped out. He started to run toward the barn.

"He's out of the car. He's running. You can shoot now," Mixell yelled at Bodine. Bodine snapped off two quick shots.

Mixell followed with another shot at the back of the fleeing man, who ran slightly crouched over. He was thankful that the Rubeck boys had left the barn and crossed the road to their home minutes before he saw the Sharpe car. They would not be caught in the crossfire.

"I think I hit him. Maybe not, I don't know. He didn't stop or change his pace," Mixell yelled. "Jeez. He's going to get away. If he makes the house, we'll never get him out," he screamed, jamming the words together. "Try to pin him down. I'm going to get help." Mixell jumped out of the ditch and sprinted to the cruiser, jerking open the door and grabbing the radio mike. "This is Carlisle No. 6. We are under fire and need help," Mixell called into the mike, looking toward the barn. He watched Bodine get off another shot at Hollenbaugh's back.

"This is the command post. Slow down and repeat your message," the officer on the other end of the radio monitored back.

Mixell just stared at the mike. He couldn't believe what he had just heard. Then in disgust he threw the mike on the front seat. Fortunately, other units were already on the air, repeating the message he had sent.

He reached over the front seat and grabbed the shotgun from the floor with his left hand, still holding the pistol in his right hand. The shotgun had been loaded earlier with five shells of buckshot.

He laid it on the seat beside him and quickly reloaded the empty revolver. Then he grabbed the heavy weapons and ran back to the ditch where Bodine was kneeling, following

Hollenbaugh's progress. "He's near the barn now, but I can't shoot. The girl is running after him and in the line of fire."

Mixell watched the girl run, now in a direct line between the officers and Hollenbaugh. As she ran, her hat fell off and her hair dropped down over her shoulders.

"Get down. Get down," Mixell yelled at her, frustrated that he was unable to do anything to stop the killer. She apparently did not hear him, because she continued to run after Hollenbaugh, cutting the distance between them with each step.

"Get down and hide," Bodine yelled at Sharpe, who was edging toward the Rubeck house. He apparently didn't hear either and he continued across the road holding his stomach. He disappeared behind the house to the north.

The five were the only people visible during the first volley of shots. The Guardsmen had done what they were told to do. When the shooting started, they hit the ditch and stayed there, empty rifles and all.

Mixell looked at Bodine. "I'm going to try to cut him off. You move up the ditch here toward the house. I'm going to go around the back and come out on the other side."

"Be careful. That S. O. B. can shoot," Bodine warned as Mixell ran off across the field to effect a collision course with Hollenbaugh.

Gasping for air, Mixell stopped short of the northeast corner of the house, where he could see the barn. He was about forty feet from the rear of it when he saw Hollenbaugh move out from under the overhang of the barn directly toward him. Calmly and with the determination that comes only when one's life is in danger, Mixell dropped to one knee, raised his pistol and shot at Hollenbaugh.

The hunted, no longer the hunter he had been with unarmed men and women, stopped, spun around in the center of the road and started running back to the barn. Mixell fired again, and Hollenbaugh fell to his knees in the middle of the road, dropping the shotgun.

From this position, Mixell could see only his back. He saw Hollenbaugh's arm draw the gun back to his body. It gave Mixell the opportunity to run behind the house to get closer and block an attempt by Hollenbaugh to get inside.

Mixell stopped at the southeast corner of the house, looked around it quickly. He saw nothing. Then he moved forward to the corner of the back porch.

During the moment he lost Hollenbaugh, his mind recorded screaming, yelling, pounding, and talking. He suddenly remembered he had not seen Sharpe, and hoped the wounded man had been admitted to the house. He hoped to God that Mary Lou had been able to escape, but he had not seen her since she and Hollenbaugh had reached the barn.

Mixell raised his head from below the porch and looked across toward the barn. This time he saw Hollenbaugh, rising to his feet on the road. He started to move toward the house again. From inside the house to his rear, he again heard screaming and pounding.

Hollenbaugh ran toward Mixell in a shuffle, like a boxer out on his feet. He carried the shotgun across his chest. His eyes glazed as he stared at and through Mixell.

When they were less than 18 feet apart, Mixell leveled the shotgun he still carried in his left hand, steadied the pistol on its barrel and aimed at Hollenbaugh's head. He wanted to be certain this time he would not miss a vital spot.

But Hollenbaugh was already sagging to his knees opposite a side window of the Rubeck home when Mixell squeezed the trigger. At the same instant, another blast shattered his eardrums from close by. Mixell thought Hollenbaugh had shot at the window, not realizing the shotgun blast had been fired from inside the house.

Hollenbaugh sank slowly, the gun still in his hands. His knees touched the ground as he fell forward, face down in the grass on the side lawn.

Mixell remained poised for thirty seconds, his weapon trained on the man who lay so still on the lawn. It seemed like five minutes before he could trust himself to move. Then he walked forward, his pistol directed at Hollenbaugh's head.

Just then, two plainclothesmen ran onto the lawn from the front of the house, their guns pointed at the fallen man.

In the background, Mixell could hear Mary Lou pounding on the back door of the Rubeck home, pleading to be let inside. She must have circled around behind the house from the opposite side, wondering numbly why the people inside would not let her in now that it was all over.

His mind also recorded the sound of a helicopter hovering in the distance, but his attention was still directed to his victim. He saw blood spilling out of Hollenbaugh.

He turned and saw two other plainclothesmen walking Mary Lou toward a car on the highway. Each had her by an arm. The girl was sobbing.

Lieutenant Tittler, who had received the urgent call for help, arrived in a cruiser and ran to the group of men, one of whom said, "Mixell shot him." Mixell removed his handcuffs from his belt and handed them to his superior officer. "I think I shot him," he reported.

Another policeman, a sergeant who joined the crowd, said, "Christ, he's dead. Why put the cuffs on him?"

Tittler spat out, "I'm in charge here and we damn sure will." He pulled Hollenbaugh's hands behind him and slipped on the cuffs.

It was over.

# THE ORDEAL

"If I live to be a hundred years old, I'll never forget how it all happened. It was a pleasant spring day, I remember, when that strange man came out of the woods. . . ."

This was Mary Lou Broderick's first glimpse of William Hollenbaugh. She and her brothers and sisters had just gotten off the school bus that Wednesday afternoon, May 11, 1966. They were ambling along the gravel road that led to their house when they saw him. He walked slowly toward them, head down. He was carrying a shotgun, which didn't seem strange to them; all the men in the area were hunters. What did seem peculiar to Mary Lou was that he was wearing motorcycle goggles. He raised his head, pointed the gun at the group and said, "Which of you little sons of bitches is going to give me any trouble?"

It was the beginning of the eight-day nightmare for the young girl.

Grabbing Mary Lou by the arm, Hollenbaugh dragged her deep into the woods, stopping only when he heard George Broderick calling to his daughter. "If you answer him," he snarled, "I'll kill you right here." Not until they had moved high up on the ridge behind the Broderick house did he stop again. It was to tell her, unemotionally, that he had planned this for a long time, and that he intended to keep her for the rest of her life. "And," he added, "you might as well get used to the idea." Almost as an after-thought, he said, "Today I was supposed to go up to a farm above your place and feed some horses, but I decided a woman was more important to me than any horses, so I waited for you instead."

She knew now that she was in the hands of a maniac. But he was a shrewd one, as she was to learn in the harrowing days ahead. "A chill went through me," she later recalled, "when I realized that he really thought he could just go out and capture a girl, just like a stray cat, and keep her at his beck and call, regardless of her feelings or her family or the police. Worst of all, he seemed to think I should be flattered by all the careful plans he had made to kidnap me. It was creepy and unreal." She resolved not to cross him because there could be no reasoning with a madman.

They walked on until they reached a clearing in the woods. Here they stopped again while he removed his goggles. He looked familiar to her but she couldn't place him. Then he put his finger in his mouth and pulled out a wire that had a piece of wood attached to each end. With the device no longer pushing his cheeks out, he looked older— and familiar. "I know who you are!" she blurted out. "You're the Bicycle Man!" Any thoughts he may have had about releasing her were gone. By recognizing him, she sealed her fate. He would never let her go.

He put the wire device into a makeshift haversack, which was already stuffed with shotgun shells, a can opener and a small transistor radio. He had even thought to include two spoons. Then he pulled off his dirty outer garments—a jacket and pants—and ordered her to put them on, to cover her red dress. She was relieved to see that he was already wearing another jacket and pants under those he had just taken off.

As they began the long trek, still moving east toward the Tuscarora Ridge, Hollenbaugh introduced himself. "My name is William Hollenbaugh. But you can call me Bill." Mary Lou remembered later that she hadn't responded with a "Glad to meet you." She kept her mouth shut. But after that, when she had to speak to him, she called him by his first name.

They hiked until nine o'clock that first night before he called a halt. While they were resting, he went over the whole business again, how he had watched her for all those months and how he had planned to get her. "Mary, you know I have taken you because I love you."

*Here it comes,* she thought. She tried to shame him. "Is this the way you show that you love someone?"

He answered, "This is the way I have to. I want sex. I never had a woman love me that way."

Her memory of that moment is still vivid. "I told him I wasn't interested in that kind of love."

He grabbed her and slapped her hard across the face, three times. "You're damned well going to get interested in it. You're going to spend the rest of your life with me and you have to face up to it some day."

Mary Lou was too frightened to fight back. She knew that if she did, the consequences could be even worse. When he finally calmed down, he began rambling, almost incoherently, about how he didn't want to make her pregnant because "we have to live in the woods and you couldn't go to a hospital and you'd probably die. All you have to do is to show me that you really love me, without actual relations. All I want is the sensation of touching a woman. I never did that." Then he pawed over her, "like somebody out of his mind," she remembers. That seemed to be all he wanted. Around ten o'clock he was distracted by car lights of the searchers. He moved Mary Lou deeper into the woods.

It wasn't until late Thursday afternoon that they stopped to rest again. Mary Lou's loafers were wearing through and her feet were covered with blisters. They had spent the day walking through the bush, out of sight of the helicopter. He rambled on most of the day, talking about himself, about his family, a brother and sister who would have nothing to do with him. "Nobody in this world ever cared for me." He talked about his house near Burnt Cabins, his three dogs. He went on and on, spilling out his grudges against the world. As it got dark, he began to worry about his dogs. Painful as it was for her, he marched the young girl the eight miles to the tarpaper shack he called "home." A short distance from the shack, he stopped to rummage through a junk pile and brought out a length of chain and a padlock. He chained her to a tree. He was back shortly; there were too many men in the vicinity. Once again, they climbed to the ridge. When they finally stopped, it was at one of his many food caches, which he had dug some time before. It was the first food Mary Lou had eaten in more than twenty-four hours.

Friday and Saturday were pain-filled blurs to the young girl. Her shoes had given out and Hollenbaugh wrapped her feet in dirty rags and gave her a pair of old galoshes to put over them. They walked continuously without rest, and she wondered if the police would ever find her. She was losing hope.

Sunday was a day to remember. Hollenbaugh was still worrying about his dogs. They hadn't been fed in three days. He and the girl worked their way across the valley, crossing Route 522, to Gobbler's Knob, close to where Hollenbaugh lived. Then, in one of his many abrupt changes of mind, he spent the rest of the day—from 10 a.m. to 6 p.m.—watching a big house he had decided to rob. While peering through his binoculars, he told Mary Lou that he was the one responsible for the attacks on Ned Price, Mary Blake, and the others. It was chilling for her to hear him say, "I had to shoot them," as if it were his God-given duty. "But I never intended to hurt nobody. I just wanted a woman."

When the spirit moved him, they headed for his shack, threading their way through and around a 600-man posse. Again, he chained her to a tree while he went to look for his dogs. In spite of the heavy surveillance, he managed to bring all three back. Two of them he sent scurrying, but one stayed with them. It was the little white dog that Terry Anderson would find and that would cause his death.

On Monday, they broke into the big house Hollenbaugh had watched for more than ten hours the day before. In spite of her own suffering, Mary Lou was sick about breaking into someone's home. She tried to talk him out of it.

He turned mean and said, "Just don't forget that when you're with me you'll do anything to get something to eat and you'll kill anybody that gets in the way. You remember that." She kept quiet.

In the house he found cartridges for a .32 automatic. "That, " Mary Lou remembers, "sent him zooming. He searched until he found the gun. When he did, he danced around me and slobbered a kiss across my face and said, 'See, if we didn't bust into this place we wouldn't have found this gun. I've been looking for this kind of gun all my life.' "

He found canned goods stored in the basement and food in the refrigerator, which he proceeded to devour. Mary Lou was too sick to eat. He found two women's suits for her. She didn't want them. All she wanted to do was wash up. He pushed her out of the house, carrying his haul in a bedsheet.

It wasn't until early Tuesday morning that Hollenbaugh found a lair that suited him, in a thick copse of pines. He was still excited by his discovery of the gun and after he had chained Mary Lou to a tree, he "made love" to her in his peculiar way—slobbering and pawing over her. Then he moved away a few yards, lay down and promptly fell asleep. Mary Lou dozed fitfully, as she had done for the past six days. She was awakened from her uneasy sleep by the barking of the little white dog and a man's voice saying, "Here, boy." She opened her eyes and saw a man's legs through the bush. It was FBI Agent Terry Anderson. Hollenbaugh was on his feet in a matter of seconds. He scooped up the shotgun and without hesitation fired at the agent. Two police dogs leapt at him and he fired twice more. Weid, then King, went down. Quickly, Hollenbaugh unchained

Mary Lou, who was in a state of shock from the sight of the carnage. They backtracked down the side of Gobbler's Knob.

The young girl was even more frightened now, with the searchers so close. Dressed in Hollenbaugh's dirty, cast-off clothes, she knew that the police could easily mistake her for her kidnapper. She had another, more immediate reason to be frightened. Somewhere along the trail, while she was wearing the chain around her neck, the padlock dropped off and was lost in the bush. When Hollenbaugh discovered the loss, he turned vicious, accusing her of deliberately losing it. Nothing she said could appease him or convince him otherwise. The more she protested, the angrier he got until finally he lashed out and hit her brutally in the face. Stunned, blood gushing from her nose, Mary Lou knew instinctively to remain quiet; any further protest would lead to more violence.

Hollenbaugh calmed down and began to think up new tactics to throw off the searchers. For the rest of that day and all of that night they worked their way through rings of searchers to Clear Ridge. They would be safe there, he assured her. It was an exhausting march for the already-tired girl, through bushes that tore at her clothes and hair, through cold, shoulder-high creek water. Toward morning, they came to Shonek's hunting lodge, where Deputy Sheriff Francis Sharpe had spent the night. When Hollenbaugh spotted Sharpe's car, he knew he had found a way out of the danger zone. He asked Mary Lou if she could drive. Thinking quickly, she answered, "No." Her lie forced Hollenbaugh to use the car's owner. He led her down to the lodge where they slipped into the outside bathroom.

It was to be the last night that Mary Lou would spend with the Bicycle Man.

Wednesday, May 18—eight days since that other horrible Wednesday—was the most terrifying day of all for the young girl. Hidden behind the shower curtain, she did not see Sharpe enter the bathroom. She only heard Hollenbaugh order Sharpe to stand still, then the report of the .32 automatic. She pushed aside the curtain and saw Sharpe, a stunned look on his face, holding his stomach. She was relieved, she said later, to find Sharpe on his feet. "I was afraid there was another dead man out there." Sharpe asked her if his wound looked bad. Before she could give him a reassuring answer, Hollenbaugh told her to shut up, then motioned them to the lodge. He made Sharpe change into his clothes, then ordered him to his car. Mary Lou followed numbly.

When the shooting started at the gate, she followed Hollenbaugh's order to run with him; she didn't know what else to do. Fright and shock made her respond with the reflexes of a prisoner. Once out in the open, her own heathy reflexes took over; she found herself running faster than her captor. She was sure that Hollenbaugh would surrender but in the meantime, she was outracing bullets.

She kept running, afraid, as she recalled, "that even if he was wounded and dying, he might shoot me." Too, she was still worried that the police might mistakenly gun her down as well. She reached the Rubecks' back door, but her pounding brought no response. Then she saw a trooper waving at her, motioning her to go on up the road. Still caught up in her fear of Hollenbaugh, she stayed where she was until she saw a group of men surround his prone figure. She ran toward the trooper—and safety.

She and Sharpe were taken in a police car to the Fulton County Medical Center, where he was treated for his gunshot wound and she had her bruises and cuts and blisters attended to.

After the ordeal was over, she spoke of Hollenbaugh. "It would be easy to say that I despise the very memory of him. I don't believe that all the misery, sorrow and death he caused was entirely his fault. It seemed to me that he was a person everybody had rejected. Apparently nobody ever took an interest in him. He was about as lonely as a human being can get. He was fighting back in the only way he could figure out, trying to capture by force the human companionship he couldn't get any other way. I just happened to be the one he caught.

# THE KIDNAPPER

William Hollenbaugh was born in Milford Township, Huntingdon County, July 24, 1921. He died in Dublin Township in adjacent Fulton County on May 18, 1966, two months before his forty-fifth birthday.

Although Hollenbaugh survived for four decades, there is pathetically little known about him. His biography consists of a series of public records, all of them grim.

In 1937, when he was 16, he, his brother, Charles, and two other young men were arrested for larceny, according to the Juniata County Criminal Court records. Their case was docketed in the December Session of Courts, listed as the *Commonwealth vs. William D. Hollenbaugh, Charles Hollenbaugh, Blair Crimmel and Daniel Coder.* On November 20, he entered a plea of guilty and was placed on probation for two years. He and his brother were to report weekly to the sheriff or his successor.

Two years later, as his probation period came to an end, he was again charged with burglary. On November 18,

1939, he entered a plea of guilty in the same court. At 18, he was no longer a youthful offender and was sentenced to a period of five to ten years in Western Penitentiary. On the same date, he pleaded guilty to a second charge of burglary and was given another five to ten years, the two sentences to run concurrently.

On all three occasions the merchandise he stole consisted of tools—saw, hammer, etc.—and even at that time the value of the items was termed "minimal."

Nothing more is known about him until, seven years later, in 1945, he was transferred from Western Penitentiary to Farview Hospital for the criminally insane at Waymart, forty-five miles northeast of Scranton. He spent the next thirteen years in the asylum.

On June 3, 1959, he was returned to Western. A month later, he was transferred to Eastern Penitentiary, and released on parole. He had just turned thirty-nine, and had spent half his life behind bars.

What happened to him from the time of his release until his abduction of Mary Lou Broderick? He didn't go to live with his family; neither his brother nor his sister would have anything to do with him. He supported himself with odd jobs, and got on the public-assistance rolls. He most likely reported to his probation officer. He had a cabin near Shade Gap, three dogs and a bicycle. It is known that he had a twenty-year grudge against the first prosecuting attorney, and that he fought with the public-assistance officials, who urged him to get a job. He was a familiar sight around Shade Gap, where he was considered a character and nicknamed "The Bicycle Man."

He was definitely a loner.

Dr. John P. Shovlin, psychiatrist at Farview Hospital, spent thirteen years with Hollenbaugh at the asylum. Contacted the day after Hollenbaugh's death, Dr. Shovlin said he "was just as surprised as anyone by Hollenbaugh's outburst." He described his former patient as "not aggressive, but a shy, meek little man who was fearful and withdrawn." When Hollenbaugh was brought to the hospital, Dr. Shovlin diagnosed him as a typical schizophrenic: "suspicious, avoiding people, fearful."

Could this "meek little man" have brutally attacked Anne Weaver, raped Mary Blake and shot Ned Price? He boasted of these crimes to Mary Lou.

Where would he have gotten the audacity to kidnap the young girl? His years of incarceration must have taken their toll on his emotional needs. Unable to identify with the rest of society—especially with women—and yet with a yearning strong enough to turn into a compulsion, the time bomb ticked away until that May afternoon while he waited for the school bus.

Dr. Shovlin shed some light on Hollenbaugh's personality when he said, "I'm not greatly surprised that Hollenbaugh became an abductor. These people are shy and backward and find it painful to associate with people of their own age."

Hollenbaugh was an emotionally bankrupt man. To obtain what he wanted—without paying the price of societal responsibility—he three times stole items of "minimal" value. In his warped mind, this must have given him a sense of self-assurance, however momentary, no matter how his actions clashed with reality. Hollenbaugh had his own "reality."

Abducting Mary Lou was an even more powerful way to get what he wanted. He did not have to observe the social amenities; he was incapable of doing so. He did not have to ask; consequently, he would not be rejected. He was not after a mature, experienced woman; he chose to kidnap a young, naive girl.

Was William Diller Hollenbaugh indeed the Mountain Man who had terrorized Burnt Cabins, Shade Gap and the surrounding areas for two years? The autopsy of his body, conducted at Kelso's Funeral Home in McConnellsburg, described Hollenbaugh as being five feet, five and three-quarters inches tall, with russet-brown hair and beard. Descriptions of the Mountain Man by his victims ran the gamut from short to very tall; young to middle-aged, prominent to hidden eyes. None of these descriptions are conclusive.

What is conclusive are the items found in and around Hollenbaugh's cabin, the disguises, such as the blocks of wood used to flesh out his cheeks and the mask and goggles he had with him when he abducted Mary Lou, and his confession to the young girl. "I had to do it," he had said. "I had to shoot them."

# EPILOGUE

It is May, 1977. More than a decade has passed since the week of horror for Mary Lou, the Brodericks, the Anderson family, and the residents of the valley.

A certain peace has returned to the area; not total tranquility, but an air of relaxation.

The Mountain Man has not yet been forgotten. There are still symbols of his reign of terror: some dormant police files are the most obvious.

The Pennsylvania Legislature has had a bill in committee since 1966. The proposed piece of legislation would have reimbursed Thomas McGinn $4500 for the loss of his prize dog, Weid. McGinn has since established a canine training center in Philadelphia.

A reward had been pledged for the capture of the Mountain Man—$3400. After Hollenbaugh's death, several people made claims for the money: Mary Blake, one of the victims (who was willing to share it with Ned Price); McGinn, the dog trainer; Larry Rubeck, the teenager who fired a shot at Hollenbaugh during the last minutes of the shoot-out; and Francis Sharpe, the deputy sheriff who had been wounded by Hollenbaugh. It was also recommended that the entire sum of money be given to the family of slain FBI agent Terry Anderson. No one received the money. The reward was all in pledges. Since Hollenbaugh was shot and killed, not brought in alive, no cash was ever received for the reward, nor was any money given out.

Several law enforcement personnel received promotions during the years. One, Grant Mixell, a religious man and an elder of his church, was advanced to sergeant in the Pennsylvania State Police.

Ned Price retired from his job and devoted his new-found leisure time to hunting and fishing in the mountains near his home.

Ken Peiffer gained worldwide acclaim for his photographs of the manhunt. His picture of McGinn grieving over the body of Weid gained him the top prize in the Pennsylvania Newspaper Publishers' Association.

Mary Lou Broderick was married a year after her abduction and has since left the area.

Bob Cox was awarded the Pulitzer Prize in Journalism for 1967 for his coverage of the kidnapping and subsequent capture of Hollenbaugh.

Many left the area—to pursue better jobs, financial security, or as one resident simply stated, "just to get away from the bad memories."

Once a year, however, during the summer, most of the people return to renew their friendships and meet at the annual Shade Gap picnic.

# APPENDIX A

Following is a list of the victims of the Mountain Man:

| | |
|---|---|
| Viola Jacka | April 6, 1964 |
| Anne Weaver | June 1, 1964 |
| Martha I. Yohn | July 1, 1964 |
| Mary Blake | August 29, 1964 |
| Ned Price | April 16, 1965 |
| Joan McMichael | May 5, 1966 |
| Mary Lou Broderick | May 11, 1966 - May 18, 1966 |

# APPENDIX B

The following is a partial list of the law enforcement personnel and local residents involved in the search for Mary Lou and her abductor:

Lieutenant Ed Mitarnowski (In charge of the search operation)
Trooper Carl F. Ruegg
Trooper Pete Migatulski
Trooper Dick Fischer
Trooper Bob Kissner
Trooper Detective Al Broscius
Captain Ed Swatij
Trooper John Laskey
Trooper Sam Kline
Trooper Ronnie Weigand
Trooper Milton Brown
Trooper Gus Alexiou
Trooper Grant Mixell
Trooper George Plafcan
Trooper Bob Derwin

Trooper Larry Herb
Trooper Ken Swider
Trooper Richard Bodine
Trooper Terry Seiple
Trooper Rocky Rockwell
Sergeant Jim Treas
Sergeant William Kimmel
Captain Ray Anderson
Lieutenant Roy Tittler
Corporal Ray Hussack
Sergeant Les Hoover
Deputy Sheriff Francis Sharpe
FBI: Joe Jamieson
      Edwin Greenwald
      John Daane
      Tom Dolan
      Terry Anderson
Dog Trainers/Handlers:
      Tom Stewart
      Thomas (Mac) McGinn
      Richard Stoud
Isaac Frehn (school bus driver)
Guy Price (brother of Ned Price)
Reporters:
      Bob Cox
      Ken Peiffer
      Gary Willhide

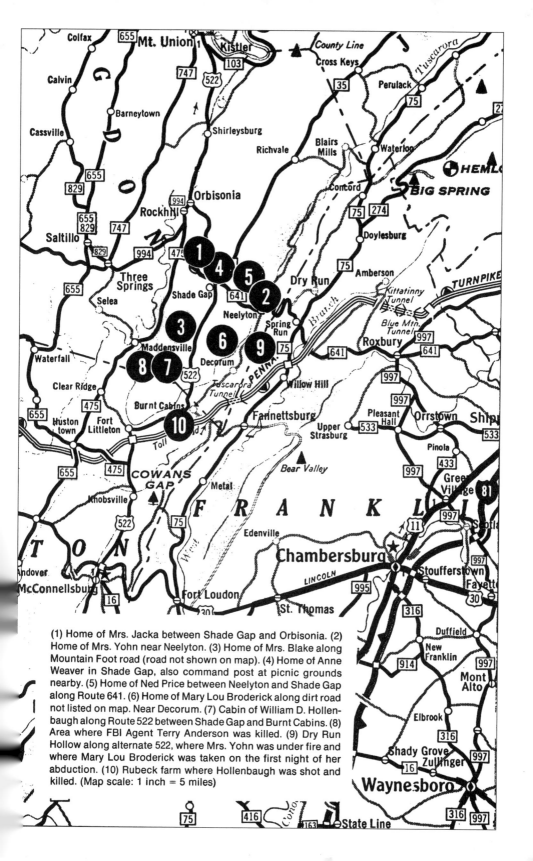

(1) Home of Mrs. Jacka between Shade Gap and Orbisonia. (2) Home of Mrs. Yohn near Neelyton. (3) Home of Mrs. Blake along Mountain Foot road (road not shown on map). (4) Home of Anne Weaver in Shade Gap, also command post at picnic grounds nearby. (5) Home of Ned Price between Neelyton and Shade Gap along Route 641. (6) Home of Mary Lou Broderick along dirt road not listed on map. Near Decorum. (7) Cabin of William D. Hollenbaugh along Route 522 between Shade Gap and Burnt Cabins. (8) Area where FBI Agent Terry Anderson was killed. (9) Dry Run Hollow along alternate 522, where Mrs. Yohn was under fire and where Mary Lou Broderick was taken on the first night of her abduction. (10) Rubeck farm where Hollenbaugh was shot and killed. (Map scale: 1 inch = 5 miles)

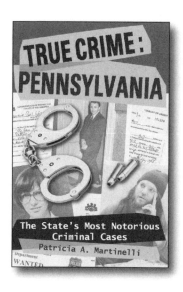